THE CHRIST

THE
CHRIST
CONUNDRUM

The Skeptic's Guide to Jesus

ANDREW CARRUTH

dangerous™
little books

First Published in Great Britain 2011 by Dangerous Little Books
www.dangerouslittlebooks.com

Contents

CONTENTS

TIMETABLE OF IMPORTANT EVENTS

INTRODUCTION   **1**

THE CHRISTIAN UNDERSTANDING OF JESUS   **5**

OBJECTIVES OF THIS BOOK   **9**
A NOTE ON THE SOURCES   12

MAKING OF THE MESSIAH   **13**
ISRAEL BEFORE THE ROMANS   15
FEATURES OF JUDAISM IN JESUS' TIME   23
RELIGIOUS TENSION UNDER THE ROMANS   28
POLITICAL AND RELIGIOUS SECTS IN THE AGE OF JESUS   32
THE GALILEANS   35
CHARISMATIC HOLY MEN   39
CONCLUSIONS   43

BIAS OF THE BIOGRAPHERS   **45**
WHAT IS A GOSPEL?   46
WHO WROTE THE GOSPELS?   49
WHEN WERE THE GOSPELS WRITTEN?   51
HOW WERE THE GOSPELS WRITTEN?   53
CAN WE KNOW ANYTHING ABOUT JESUS' CHARACTER FROM
THE GOSPELS?   56
WHY DOES JESUS RIDE TWO DONKEYS?   60
ARE THE GOSPELS FOR OR AGAINST JEWISH LAW?   64
CONCLUSIONS   68

WHEN GOD IS A CHILD   **71**
WAS JESUS DESCENDED FROM DAVID?   73
THE GENEALOGY OF JESUS ACCORDING TO MATTHEW   74
THE GENEALOGY OF JESUS ACCORDING TO LUKE   74
WAS MARY REALLY A VIRGIN?   78
WAS JESUS BORN IN BETHLEHEM OR NAZARETH?   84
WHAT IS IT LIKE BEING A CHILD GOD?   88
WHY DOES JESUS' FAMILY THINK HE IS MAD?   91
WHAT HAPPENED TO JESUS' BROTHER?   93
CONCLUSIONS   98

WHAT JESUS REALLY TAUGHT   **99**

How Did Jesus Teach?   101
Was Jesus Really A Jew?   103
What Did Jesus Wear?   106
Why Does Jesus Fight With The Pharisees?   107
Did Jesus Believe The End of The World Was Near?   111
Was Jesus A Failed Prophet?   117
How Should We Follow Jesus?   119
Was Jesus The Messiah?   121
Did Jesus Say That He Was The Son of God?   125
Conclusions   128

THE MEANING OF MIRACLES   **131**

What Miracles Did Jesus Supposedly Perform?   132
What Were The Ancient Causes And Treatments Of
Diseases?   134
Could Jesus Miraculously Heal People?   138
Could Jesus Exorcise Demons?   141
What Does Jesus' Control Over Nature Symbolize?   144
Could Jesus Raise The Dead?   148
How Unique Are Jesus' Miraculous Abilities?   151
Conclusions   157

HIS EXECUTION AND RESURRECTION   **159**

How Did Jesus Die?   162
Why Do The Soldiers Want Jesus' Underwear?   166
Why Did Jesus Die?   168
Was Pontius Pilate Innocent Or Guilty Of Killing
Jesus?   170
Why Were The Jews Blamed For Killing Jesus?   172
Did Jesus Really Rise From The Dead?   175
Conclusions   181

HOW JESUS BECAME GOD   **183**

What Did The First Disciples Believe?   185
How Did The Faith Spread?   187
Who Was Paul of Tarsus?   191
Did Paul Think Jesus Was God?   196
What Was Paul's Understanding of Jesus?   198
When Did Jesus First Become Divine?   203

WHAT WAS PAUL'S INFLUENCE ON ALTERNATIVE
CHRISTIANITIES?   206
WHAT DID THE JEWISH CHRISTIANS THINK ABOUT PAUL?   211
HOW WAS THE BATTLE OF FAITH WON?   214
WHAT FACTORS CONTRIBUTED TO THE VICTORY?   217
CONCLUSIONS   221

THE EVOLUTION OF FAITH   **223**

RECOMMENDED READING

Timetable of Important Events

Before Current Era

- 722 Assyria conquers Jerusalem and deports the population
- 586 Babylonians conquer Jerusalem and destroy Solomon's temple
- c. 532 Persians conquer Babylon and allow exiled Jews to return. The temple is re-built
- 332 Alexander the Great conquers Judea.
- 167 Maccabean revolt sparked by Antiochus' pagan rituals at the temple
- 141 Hasmonean family rules the independent Jewish kingdom
- 63 Roman General Pompey conquers Jerusalem and Hasmoneans become client kings of Rome
- 37 King Herod's rule is established
- 6-4 Jesus is born

Current Era

- 6 Rome annexes Judea, Samaria and Idumea and incorporated the region into its province of Syria. A census for tax purposes sparks revolt under Judah the Galilean.
- 26-36 Pontius Pilate is prefect of Judea
- c. 28 Jesus meets John the Baptist and begins his public ministry
- c. 30-32 Jesus is executed
- 35-36 Paul is on the road to Damascus
- c. 39 Caligula attempts to put a statue of himself in the Temple which sparks Jewish mass protests.
- c. 44-46 Theudas is beheaded by Roman Procurator Fadus for saying he would part the river Jordan
- c. 48 Council of Jerusalem. Paul argues against circumcision.

- c. 51-64 Paul writes his famous epistles
- c. 55 The Egyptian and his followers are massacred by the Romans.
- c. 58 Paul is arrested, later sent to Rome
- 62 James the Just is stoned to death
- 64 Great Fire of Rome
- c. 65-70 Mark writes his gospel
- 66-68 Revolt against Romans and Jerusalem besieged – The First Jewish War.
- 70 Jerusalem is sacked by victorious Romans and the Temple is destroyed.
- c. 80-100 Josephus writes his two most famous works, the Jewish War and the Jewish Antiquities
- c. 80-85 Matthew writes his gospel
- c. 85-90 Luke writes his gospel
- c. 90-100 John writes his gospel
- 132-135 Bar Kokhba Revolt – The Second Jewish War.
- 235-311 Persecution of Christians in various regions of the Empire
- 313 Christianity legalized by the Edict of Milan
- 325 Council of Nicaea

Introduction

"But if it is preached that Christ has been raised from the dead, how can some of you say that there is no resurrection of the dead? If there is no resurrection of the dead, then not even Christ has been raised. And if Christ has not been raised, our preaching is useless and so is your faith." - 1 Corinthians 15:12-14

If we believed everything Christians told us about Jesus then we would have to conclude that the Son of God has a split personality. On the one hand, Jesus is a source of comfort, a proverbial shoulder to cry on – a big brother in the sky who taught mankind about forgiveness and love. On the other, he is a strict moral teacher who at the end of time will sit at the right hand of God and judge us of our sins. Those who did not heed his message will be condemned to eternal damnation in a fiery hell.

Instead, it seems that Christians choose to interpret Jesus according to their own needs. Jesus can mean just about anything to anyone. For example, Jesus was the figurehead of the Christian Communist movement since he framed his mission to the poor, and in the Bible he said that the rich would find it impossible to enter the Kingdom of God. Meanwhile, the feminist movement emerging out of the nineteenth century also claimed Jesus as their own. After all, women walked alongside Jesus and were the first to witness the resurrected Christ.

Today there are over two billion Christians worldwide, in hundreds of denominations representing people from every nation, continent, race and creed. Some are happy to praise him in quiet contemplation and silent prayer, while others feel the need to cross the globe and preach the gospel to primitive societies in the most inaccessible parts of the world. Great deeds of charity have been performed in the name of Jesus, but at the same time some of the most gruesome acts of violence have been unleashed because of it. We are able to read into Jesus whatever we like and this has led to some contrasting and contradictory understandings of Jesus.

What unites Christians is a common belief that two millennia ago, God assumed human form and walked upon the earth. And Christians claim this is no mere myth; Jesus' tale takes place in historical times and in historical places. Indeed, the gospels are full of names, places, people and events which we can check against other historical data to confirm or deny. For example, the gospels (the biographies of Jesus if you like) tell us that Jesus interacted with Pontius Pilate, who we know existed because we have archaeological and textual evidence independent of the Christian tradition that supports this. Most scholars, therefore, conclude that a man called Jesus did actually exist.

In the eighteenth century, some scholars embarked on what is known as the quest for the historical Jesus. This was an attempt to sift through all the historical sources and seek to understand Jesus as he was in his own time. It was reasoned that Jesus could be known through historical method rather than through faith alone. However, it became quickly apparent that even the supposedly objective historian could warp Jesus into something he was not. In the past, the historical Jesus has been reconstructed as a Jewish patriotic rebel with a political agenda, the Che Guevara of his day. Other scholars have seen Jesus as a roving holy man, a faith healer and a magician.

Recently, the quest has benefited from several new lines of evidence. For one thing, the discovery of a library of texts amid the Egyptian desert at Nag Hammadi in 1945 gave us a brand new understanding of some early

Christian sects from the third century that have since become extinct. Furthermore, the Dead Sea scrolls discovered at Qumran in 1949 allowed historians an unprecedented glimpse into the life of one Jewish sect in the era shortly before Jesus' birth. More importantly, however, the quest for the historical Jesus has made some intriguing progress thanks to a broader acceptance of historical methodology and an understanding that historians are just as apt to bias their reconstruction of Jesus as any Christian. These days it is accepted that the historian must be as objective as possible when approaching the historical Jesus. They must distance themselves from the modern world and actively seek to place themselves in the mindset of a first century Jew. They must forget centuries of Christian dogma and doctrine and search for Jesus within his own time. When this is done then the Jesus of history starts to emerge; Jesus was a Jew, he preached to his fellow Jews and had a very Jewish message. Needless to say, interpreting Jesus according to history is not without controversy, mainly because Jesus and his teaching are distinctly unchristian.

We do know a few solid things about the life of the historical Jesus, which both Christians and historians generally agree upon. Firstly, Jesus was born shortly before the death of Herod the Great sometime around 4 - 6 BCE. He spent most of his life in and around a small village called Nazareth in the rural province of the Galilee but at some stage he met John the Baptist, an important religious figure of this era. John baptizes Jesus in the river Jordan and afterwards Jesus begins his own public ministry. He recruits a band of followers, known as the disciples, and over the next few years wanders through the Galilee healing other Jews through faith and teaching them about the 'Kingdom of God.' Eventually, possibly around 30 CE, Jesus leaves his native territory and heads to Jerusalem in the province of Judea, which was then ruled by the Romans. At the great Temple he causes some kind of disturbance. The Gospels say he overturned the pigeon seller's stalls. After a final meal with his twelve disciples, Temple authorities arrest Jesus. Probably, he is interrogated by the high priest of the Temple or by a council of judges but eventually he is handed over to the Roman overseer of Judea, Pontius Pilate, and is executed by crucifixion. But his death is not the end of the story.

The disciples who had fled at the first sign of trouble soon experience Jesus again in some manner. They claim to have found Jesus' empty tomb and witnessed the risen Jesus. Shortly after, the first Christians continue preaching based on the understanding that Jesus was the messiah predicted in the Jewish scriptures and that he had been raised up from the dead.

This brief sketch of the Jesus story will allow us a framework to work with during the course of this book. These few facts are the basis of Jesus' historical life but are also used by Christians to evidence something all together different.

The Christian Understanding of Jesus

Christians believe that Jesus was an historical person but they also understand him to be something much greater than a mere man. Jesus is God. This view is best summed up by the Apostle's Creed, variations of which are recited by many Christian denominations today:

> "I believe in God, the Father almighty, creator of heaven and earth. I believe in Jesus Christ, God's only Son, our Lord, who was conceived by the Holy Spirit, born of the Virgin Mary, suffered under Pontius Pilate, was crucified, died, and was buried; he descended into hell. On the third day he rose again; he ascended into heaven, he is seated at the right hand of the Father, and he will come to judge the living and the dead. I believe in the Holy Spirit, the holy Catholic Church, the communion of saints, the forgiveness of sins, the resurrection of the body, and the life everlasting. Amen."

The creed represents all of the basic beliefs of Christianity rolled into one simple statement. Clearly, it alludes to Jesus being a historical person when it mentions Pontius Pilate, but there are many additional theological notions incorporated within it. The creed mentions the Father, the Son and the Holy Spirit (also known as the Holy Ghost). These three concepts are known collectively as the Trinity. According to this idea, God is one single entity comprising of three distinct aspects. One of these aspects is Jesus himself who is the Son of the Father. Through the Holy Spirit, the father selected a human woman of outstanding virtue and made her pregnant and so the Virgin Mary gave birth to Jesus. Thus, Jesus is understood to have been both a human being and a divine, omniscient entity at the same time. Christians believe that Jesus is God.

They also believe Jesus' life was predicted centuries previously by certain Jewish prophets who foresaw the day when God would send the messiah to the earth. The Jews had expected the messiah to be a direct descendent of the fabled king David (the same David who defeated the goliath) and therefore Christians believe that the human Jesus did have the correct bloodline to fulfill this role. The Jewish term 'messiah' when translated into Greek becomes 'Khristos' from whence derives the name Jesus Christ.

Why should God bother sending an aspect of himself to humankind? Jesus didn't descend merely to impress us with his miraculous ability, say Christians, because Jesus also bought an important message. Humanity must repent its sins, love one another and have faith in God are but three Christian interpretations of why God entered into human form. Perhaps the most crucial element of Jesus' existence was to forgive us our sins, say Christians.

Sin is defined as humanity's refusal to follow God's moral laws. Since adultery is expressly forbidden by God, for example, should we engage in this act we are considered to be in a state of sin. Being a sinner means that we are essentially further away from God. And since the human soul always aspires to be close to the creator, Jesus by forgiving our sins is actually bringing us closer to God. Jesus died to cleanse humanity of sin, an expression which is found in the Gospel of John:

> *"This is love: not that we loved God, but that he loved us and sent his Son as an atoning sacrifice for our sins."*[1]

---

[1] 1 John 4:10

Although Jesus died two thousand years ago, Christians can still read about his message and hope to gain salvation because there is a certain collection of holy books. The New Testament comprises some twenty seven books supposedly written by men who had either known Jesus in his own lifetime or who had known some of the original apostles of Jesus. The most relevant of these for studying the life of Jesus, for both Christians and historians alike, are the four gospels, said to have been written by men named Matthew, Mark, Luke and John. The gospels contain a wealth of information about the life of Jesus and because they are set in historical times and places they have often been described as biographies. Also important to Christians are the letters (known as Epistles) of Paul of Tarsus. Paul, who lived from approximately 5 BCE to 67 CE, is the earliest Christian writer and one of the first missionaries active in the first century in spreading the 'good news' of Jesus. Although Paul had never known Jesus personally during his lifetime, Paul claims to have experienced the resurrected Christ and therefore his epistles are an additional way to understand Jesus and God. Paul's letters are also valuable to the historian because they allow such a unique insight into the very dawn of Christianity.

Objectives of This Book

This book will proceed with the premise that it is possible to know something of the Jesus of history. Jesus has often been described, quite rightly, as a Jew. He was a man who did have a historical message that appealed to his Jewish contemporaries. But this historical Jew was not God. He simply could not be. As a Jew, he would have found it blasphemous for men to proclaim himself as a deity. And this is the real conundrum, how could someone who was hailed as a 'rabbi' by his own people come to hold such exalted status? How did a historical Jew come to be hailed as a deity? How did a simple human being come to be regarded as an omniscient God?

This book shall attempt to answer this conundrum but will proceed with three specific objectives in mind:

(a) To undermine Christian notions that Jesus is God by

(b) understanding how he came to be proclaimed God in the first place, which will be achieved though

(c) reconstructing the life and teachings of the historical Jesus as his contemporaries would have known him.

To understand the real Jesus we must understand the world in which he lived and taught. We shall, therefore, examine Jewish history and religion preceding the life of Jesus. This will allow us to understand how and why Jesus came to be heralded as the messiah; why he ended up hanging from the cross; and it will also make it possible to see Jesus as a recognizably first century Jew.

To further understand Jesus, we also have to examine the gospels. The sources dealing with his life will be demonstrated to be theologically motivated, that is they were written by men who want us to believe that Jesus

9

was the messiah. However, by treating the gospels just like any historical source we can comb them for reliable information about Jesus which should fit in with what we know about the world in which he lived.

Through understanding Jesus' Jewish context and the historical sources dealing with his life, it will be demonstrated that many aspects of Jesus' life (the claim he was a descendent of David, that his mother was a virgin and that he fulfilled the Jewish prophecies) are mere Christian innovation. Instead we can build a historically plausible understanding of Jesus and reconstruct what he actually taught his contemporaries and what he really taught should also match what we know about his original context.

What will become apparent is that Jesus really was a radical - his followers left their wives and children to follow Jesus based on an understanding that the world was about to end within their lifetimes.

Placing ourselves in the mindset of the ancients will also help us to provide a secular explanation for Jesus' miraculous abilities. Jesus was said to have healed the sick, exorcised demons and controlled the forces of nature. But when we remember that the ancients did not perceive the world in scientific terms these can easily be explained away. Indeed the ancient world is filled with many examples of miracle workers and if anything Jesus seems to fit into a familiar pattern of other similar men from the first century.

Jesus' death is the most haunting episode from the gospels, and just why he died shall be examined. The gospels say he was killed because his fellow Jews had plotted to kill him, but this shall be demonstrated to be historically implausible. Most likely, Jesus died because the Romans regarded him as a troublemaker during a politically sensitive time.

Shortly after his death, the disciples witness the risen Jesus. This leads them to continue preaching. But what historical evidence lies behind the claim that Jesus lived again? Did they actually see him again? Or are there other explanations? Once again, understanding the mindset of the 'witnesses' will allow us to show that Jesus did not really rise from the dead.

Ultimately, through this reasoning it will be shown that Jesus was not a God at all. Indeed as a pious and monotheistic Jew, he would have been disgusted that generations of Christians have worshipped him as an omniscient being. Christians have taken his story out of context and made it into something it could not have possibly been.

As may have been gathered already, this book is written from a skeptical perspective. The author in fact is an atheist who professes no religious belief. So why should a skeptic want to dismiss the divine Christ? Why not leave the Christian faith as it is? Why risk upsetting sensibilities merely to make a historical point?

This book is written to promote reason, something that is unfortunately lacking in much of a world dominated by faith in ancient fables and superstitions. Reason can also be applied to Jesus and Christianity. When critical and methodological history is used to deconstruct the myth of Jesus, it becomes evident that the only thing holding together Christianity is faith. Faith, unlike reason, does not require evidence. Faith is subjective and personal. And where one faith meets another there is conflict, and more often than not, bloodshed. Although one faith can unite community or nation it can never unite humanity. And as we live in an increasingly globalised arena, we should, therefore, seek to find a common understanding – this is something reason can achieve but where faith falls flat.

There has in recent years been a wealth of books promoting atheism. Despite some brilliant arguments however, many continue to cling onto their superstitious beliefs that a two thousand year old peasant is actually the creator of the universe. Hopefully, by examining Jesus though the lens of reason, and by using the gospels as a tool to remove Jesus' divinity rather than supporting it, more and more otherwise intelligent people can come to accept the truth of the matter and accept reason over faith as a better tool for comprehending our world.

A Note On The Sources

In this book the New International Version (NIV) of the bible is quoted purely for the ease of reading that the translation allows for the lay reader, although it should be noted that serious students are recommended to use the Revised Standard Version (RSV) for the accuracy of the words to the original meaning. For example, the RSV mentions 'Hades' and 'Sheol' which the NIV translates merely as 'hell.' Meanwhile, it should be noted that today secular historians tend to use the appellations 'CE' meaning current era and 'BCE' meaning before the current era instead of the traditional BC and AD when discussing dates because of the obvious religious connotations they bring to a work. The dates are the same in both systems however.

CHAPTER ONE

Making of The Messiah

Some two thousand years ago there once walked on this earth a man known as Jesus. It was recorded that Jesus roamed the streets of Jerusalem prophesying that the city was doomed, *"Woe, woe to Jerusalem,"* was his call. Eventually, however, the people tired of his visions of cataclysm and he was arrested and handed over to the Roman rulers. In their own particular style of governance, the Romans gave Jesus such harsh flogging that his bones were exposed to the dry desert air, but thinking him to be nothing but a mad man they released him. Jesus' brush with the authorities did not however deter him from his adamant cries of destruction.

Alas, Jesus' prediction was to prove correct. Within a few years the might of the Roman imperial legions were assembled outside Jerusalem's walls to crush a Jewish rebellion. Their mighty siege engines flung huge boulders at the walls, killing Jesus in the process, and eventually they succeeded in taking the city in what is referred to as the First Jewish War (66-70 CE).

This story is interesting for numerous reasons, and anyone with a brief understanding of the better-known 'Jesus Christ' might be forgiven for having seen striking similarities between the two. Both of these men had called to the people with prophecies of destruction for Jerusalem – Jesus Christ had predicted that not a stone would be left of the great Temple during his own ministry several years before. Both of these men were to have a run in with the ruling Roman authorities who disliked troublemakers. Both these men were punished in Jerusalem.

The above story of Jesus Bar Abbas comes handed down to us from the Jewish chronicler Josephus (37-100 CE), who is the historian's most useful witness of these times, having participated in the First Jewish War as a commander defending the city of Jotopata. By his own story, Josephus is trapped in a cave with forty of his countrymen and surrounded by Roman troops. The situation becomes hopeless and the trapped Jews decide that suicide is the best option. They draw lots to determine who would kill who, but for some reason Josephus survives; whether by luck of the draw or by some desire to survive we cannot know. He promptly surrenders himself to the Roman commander Titus Flavius Vespasianus (9 – 79 CE), better known to history as Vespasian.

Finding himself in a sticky situation, Josephus is perhaps pandering to his captor's ego when he applies an ancient prophecy to Vespasian – the ruler of the world would one day emerge from Judea. As it happened, Vespasian would be crowned Emperor of Rome three years later and he would consequently reward Josephus handsomely with land in Judea, a substantial pension and Roman citizenship.

Now under the patronage of the Flavian family, Josephus writes a history of the Jewish War and a history of the Jewish people – his two most well known works. Though highly biased in favor of the Romans, Josephus gives us the best history we have of first century Israel and he also mentions Jesus and Jesus' brother James as well as other religious figures of the day, John the Baptist among them.

Drawing on Josephus' work and other textual evidence we can thus construct a world in which 'Jesus Christ' lived and operated. Having a firm understanding of this background information means we are in a better position to understand Jesus himself, therefore in this chapter, we shall paint a brief picture of the history of Israel. It will help us to understand how a humble Jewish teacher came to be pronounced king of the Jews, and later came to be understood as God of the universe.

Israel Before The Romans

The history of the Israelites is provided in the first several books of the Old Testament, which, of course, means it is shrouded in myth and mystery. Although secular historians reject these books as such, the Jews of Jesus' age nevertheless understood the characters and events of the scriptures to be totally historical. The most important man from this past was Moses.

According to the Book of Exodus, all of the Hebrew people were enslaved in Egypt. Being favored by God, the Jewish slaves begin to multiply causing the Pharaoh to see them as an emerging threat to his power. He commands all newborn Hebrew male children to be drowned in the river Nile. Moses should have been killed at his birth but his mother saves him by placing him in a basket and floating him down the river where he is discovered by the Pharaoh's daughter. Feeling pity for the child, she pays a Hebrew woman to nurse the infant unaware that the chosen maid is Moses' actual mother and that the child is destined for greatness.

When Moses is fully grown, God speaks to him through the most extraordinary of mediums, a burning bush. He commands Moses to lead his people out from slavery and towards a land of milk and honey. After many trials and tribulations, Moses leads them eastwards, famously parting the seas to allow his people a safe passage to freedom and drowning the pursuing Egyptian forces behind them.

Eventually, Moses is called on by God to ascend Mount Sinai, where over a period of forty days and forty nights he is alone until God provides him with the Ten Commandments. For this reason, Moses has been known by Jews ever since as the lawgiver. Led by Moses and given the responsibility of carrying the Ark of the Covenant, in which the Ten Commandments were kept and where God was thought to reside, the Jews wandered the desert before settling on the land promised to them by God. After warring with and ultimately slaughtering the local Philistine culture the Jews settle down.

According to the scriptures, the Jews at this time were divided into twelve tribes and live in a confederacy of sorts overseen by charismatic leaders called Judges. They are finally united into one kingdom by the semi-mythical figure of King David. David, the greatest Jewish king, united the tribes under one monarchy and ushered in a golden age for the Jews. He established Jerusalem as his capital and the kingdom thrived. David was also favored by God and according to the Old Testament his offspring would establish an everlasting kingdom:

> *"The LORD declares to you that the LORD himself will establish a house for you: When your days are over and you rest with your fathers, I will raise up your offspring to succeed you, who will come from your own body, and I will establish his kingdom. He is the one who will build a house for my Name, and I will establish the throne of his kingdom forever."* [2]

Perhaps God had tired of living in the Ark for so long when he commanded David's son and successor, King Solomon, to build an impressive new temple to reside in. Historically speaking, the first Temple was likely constructed around 960 BCE.

---

[2] 2 Samuel 11-13

Solomon, however, was not as pious as his father and he turned away from God and began to worship idols – the worst sin for a monotheistic Jew. As a direct consequence of his sins, the kingdom splits into two, the northern kingdom of Israel with its capital in Samaria and the southern Kingdom of Judah with its capital in Jerusalem. From henceforward the Jews would look forward to a time when God would unite the Israelites once again.

History has shown that the kingdoms of Israel had always attracted the attention of foreign empires. First of all came the Assyrians (originating in modern day Iraq) who in 722 BCE trampled over Israel in order to get their hands on the fertile Nile delta in Egypt. In order to preserve the peace in conquered territories the Assyrians favored a policy of forced migrations. The idea was that displaced persons were less likely to rebel against their leadership. Consequently, the traditional twelve tribes of Israel were left in disarray when ten tribes from the northern kingdom were taken away. Despite this, the Jews would always remember that there had once been twelve tribes and would dream of God's intervention to reunite them again. The Assyrians clung to power in the region for a century before being wiped away by the remerging empire of the Babylonians.

Once again, a foreign empire had its eye on the rich Egyptian lands and once again the Jewish kingdoms were in the way. When the Judeans sided with the Egyptians against the Babylonians they had chosen the wrong side. Their armies were defeated and the city of Jerusalem was besieged. The great Temple itself was destroyed in 586 BCE.

Many of the Judean elite were exiled and settled in the Babylonian empire. Both the Assyrian and Babylonian invasions would see Jews dispersed around the region. This marks the beginning of the Jewish Diaspora (meaning a scattering) and from this moment onwards there would be communities of Jews spread around the cities of the known world.

Though they were to settle down to raise crops and families, the exile was understood to be a punishment from God. The Jews, the chosen people of Yahweh, had been unfaithful to the jealous deity and the exile was a consequence of it. Prophets such as Ezekiel dreamed that if the Jews would repent and follow God then their homeland would be restored to them. The exiled Jews would finally find their freedom when another power in the region rose. The Persian Empire swallowed the Babylonians in 540 BCE.

King Cyrus II (circa 576 – 530 BCE) was lenient towards the Jews who had been exiled by the Babylonians and allowed them to return to the lands of their fathers. Cyrus was generous enough to subsidize their return and provided monies for their rebuilding efforts. The returning Jews were even able to re-construct their temple.

At any rate, these events are significant in the development of Jewish history and serve to illustrate an important point; the Jews thought that because of idolatry and sin they had been punished with exile. But with repentance they would be redeemed. In other words, God used military powers and foreign empires to forge his will on earth.

Meanwhile, across the seas the Greeks had long dreamed of conquering Persia. Under a young and pretentious General, the Macedonians would realize the Greek ambition. Alexander the Great swept through the region with speed and fury, defeating his enemies and conquering Israel in 333 BCE. But Alexander's empire, like his life, was short lived. After Alexander's death his commanders fought for what they could get and one of them, Seleucid, would take control of vast swathes of Alexander's eastern empire including Israel. From now on Greek culture would permeate the region, influencing Jewish politics and religion in a process called Hellenization.

Hellenization of the region meant that Jerusalem soon sported theatres and gymnasiums as well as other staples of Greek culture. Furthermore, it meant that Hellenic influence crept into the Jewish religion. The Jewish scriptures were translated into Greek and some thinkers would seek to find congruence between Jewish monotheism and Greek philosophy. Many Jews, especially within the Diaspora, would have been highly influenced by this ongoing process, but the results were not always harmonious.

A later Seleucid king, Antiochus (215 – 164 BCE) eventually forbade the traditional Jewish religious worship in favor of the pagan Hellenistic rites in 167 BCE. He sought to re-dedicate the Jewish Temple to Zeus, the king of the Greek pantheon of gods. To many Jews, this was a terrible fate. The laws handed down to them by God, via his emissary Moses, strictly forbade worshipping idols. And since Yahweh was a jealous God, worshipping other deities was a horrible sin. A guerrilla uprising, known as the Maccabean revolt, erupted in Judea under Mattathias of the Hasmonean family and lasted for three years. Some scholars interpret the revolt as a civil war between the Hellenized reformist Jews and the traditional orthodox Jews.

The orthodox Jews were to win. Upon their victory, the Temple was ritually cleansed and the holiday of Hanukkah still celebrated today commemorates this moment. The Hasmoneans established a ruling dynasty of Judea that would last for a century. At last, a Jewish king was again in charge and quickly the kingdom was expanded. Non-Jews in neighboring Idumea were told to convert or leave and the province was incorporated into the kingdom. In the eyes of the victors it seemed that God had been on the side of the pious and through his will the Jews were strong again.

Freedom was short lived, however. By the time that the Temple was being cleansed the Roman republic was already growing strong. By 100 BCE Rome's territorial expansion encompassed much of the Mediterranean including modern day Spain, southern France, Greece, parts of Turkey and North Africa. But they would not stop there. Spearheaded by ambitious military commanders the expansion would continue and like its predecessors Rome had its sights set on the Nile delta.

Sweeping through the region in 65-63 BCE, General Pompey destroyed the last remnant of the Seleucid Empire hanging on in Antioch. Pompey found the small Jewish kingdom of Judea fractured between two warring Hasmonean brothers, Hyrcanus and Aristobulus, who both craved power for themselves. In typical Roman style, Pompey sided with one and cast the other out. Reasoning that the weaker of the two would make a more grateful ally of Rome, Pompey sided with Hyrcanus and sent Aristobulus to Rome as a prisoner. Hyrcanus was not granted kingship of Judea but was instead installed as the high priest of the Temple. This was an important position but at that moment lacked political power. Rome intended to call the shots from now on but their plans would be thwarted.

As it happened, Hyrcanus was deposed by his nephew Antigonus. In 40 BCE, Antigonus allied himself with the Roman's arch enemy, the Parthians, and bit off his uncle's ear so that he could never serve as high priest again (the high priest was supposed to be unblemished to serve God). Of course, the Romans did not look fondly on someone who had upset their plans and consequently sought someone who could remove this upstart. Herod was their man.

Herod (74 BCE – 4 BCE) had come to Rome to bolster his own desire to rule, the senate backed him and proclaimed him king of the Jews in 40 BCE, supporting him with troops in his conquest of Judea. Three years later, Herod, with Roman help, would succeed in taking Jerusalem. Antigonus was executed and along with him the Hasmonean dynasty disappeared forever.

Although there is no corroborating evidence of Herod's infamous massacre of the innocents mentioned only in the gospel of Matthew, Herod was nevertheless known for his fondness of executing members of his own family. He murdered his wife and her mother, a couple of brothers in law, and three of his own sons. Later historians would reflect on the paranoia and madness of his kingship.

Needless to say, the Jewish population was soon weary of Herod. In their eyes, he had removed the legitimate kings of the Hasmonean dynasty. Moreover, he was responsible for ending the kingdom's brief independent rule, and once again the Jews were under control of a foreign empire. And well, he wasn't a full Jew! Herod's descendents were from Idumea and the king was merely a second generation convert to Judaism. As such, he was not eligible to hold the position of high priest (although he made sure his own favorites were installed in this role.)

From a Roman perspective, Herod was a good ruler. He was strong enough to maintain law and order and he kept the taxes coming in. Besides this, he was responsible for a great number of building projects in the region. Inspired by Greco-Roman culture, he built theatres, amphitheatres and maybe also a hippodrome for chariot races. He constructed shimmering palaces and grandiose public buildings and even founded a Hellenistic city in honor of the Roman Emperor called Caesarea Maritima which was famous for the sheer audacity and engineering skill of its harbor. Much of Herod's work can still be seen today.

Herod is best known for his work renovating the great Temple at Jerusalem which he completed in grandiose manner. This structure was so large that it attracted foreign tourists who would stand in awe at the massive steps, the giant looming archways and the solid, impenetrable walls. For these reasons he was known as Herod the Great.

His reign wasn't without the occasional religious blunder, however. Towards the end of his life, Herod placed a golden eagle over the gate of the Temple. This was a gesture of friendliness to the Roman rulers but to Jewish eyes it was an absolute affront to their traditional worship. The eagle was idolatrous and might have reminded them of the Seleucid attempts to Hellenize the temple. It was torn down by angry Jews whom Herod promptly executed.

Herod died shortly afterward, succumbing to a terrible disease that saw his groin infested with worms –his enemies understood this as a fitting punishment from God and a direct result of his idolatrous eagle. His kingdom was split between three of his sons. Herod Archelaus took over Judea and was at once confronted with the aftermath of his father's golden blunder. A group of Jews assembled to honor those executed by Herod over the eagle incident, but Archelaus had them all killed.

By 6 CE, the Roman Emperor Augustus had removed Archelaus, most likely because of his inflammatory actions towards his own people. Rome wanted peaceful provinces because they generally generated more cash and Archelaus' massacre of his subjects was not good for profits. The Romans decided to place Judea under direct rule and incorporated it into their existing province of Syria. By the time Jesus visited Judea, the province was firmly under Roman control.

Features of Judaism in Jesus' Time

The Jews of this period were largely concerned with following as best as they could the laws as laid down to them by the prophet Moses. To the western mind, Moses is best remembered for the Ten Commandments. Moreover, according to first century Jews, Moses had also written the Torah, which are the first five books of the Old Testament; Genesis, Exodus, Leviticus, Numbers, and Deuteronomy. Later Rabbinic sources would identify more than ten general rules – in fact there are over six hundred mitzvoth, or commandments contained within the Torah itself. Everything from the correct method of sacrifice to forbidding the skin to be tattooed, from when to observe the Sabbath and rules concerning loaning money – everything is covered in the Torah. The Jews of Jesus' age, and indeed Jews ever since, revere the Torah as God's commandments and to follow them is to lead a good and holy life.

The commandments contained within the Torah are also known as the Mosaic Law because they are understood to have been written by Moses (although scholars generally dispute this). Infringement of the law could entail capital punishment for serious offences such as blasphemy or, for lesser crimes, an atoning animal or grain sacrifice could be offered at the Temple. A few important features of the law will be of direct relevance to us when we try to understand Jesus and the early church so the most important commandments for our study will be briefly described here.

Kosher laws are primarily stated in the books of Numbers and Deuteronomy and describe which animals are lawful to eat and which are not. To this day, Jews refuse to eat pork based on the Mosaic Law and this was true of first century Israelites too. Generally speaking, it was permissible to eat any creature with a cloven hoof but the correct method of sacrifice had to be observed. The creature was to be drained of its blood since God had prohibited its consumption:

"Any Israelite or any alien living among them who eats any blood – I will set my face against that person who eats blood and will cut him off from his people."[3]

Jews living in the Diaspora would have had to be particularly careful when dining with pagans. Their Gentile (that is non-Jewish) neighbors did not observe Kosher, Pork was a popular dish for example, and so eating with the Gentiles was generally frowned upon.

Another interesting feature of Mosaic Law is circumcision. According to Genesis, God had instructed Abraham to be circumcised as a covenant between him and his chosen people. The Romans thought this nothing less than a horrific form of self torture and frowned upon it. When Christianity began to spread beyond its Jewish roots, there was considerable debate among followers as to whether they were bound by Jewish law and therefore commanded to be circumcised, but Jews of Jesus' age almost universally practiced removing the foreskin from their male children.

And finally, the Jews observed the Sabbath. Even God had needed a day of rest and therefore humans were allowed one too. This wasn't an option however, it was a commandment. There was to be no work done whatsoever on the day of Sabbath. Not even a pot of

---

[3] Leviticus 17:10

soup was allowed to be cooked and indeed all preparation of food occurred the day before. The Gentiles who worked everyday regarded their Jewish neighbors as simply being lazy.

Perhaps the most difficult concept of Judaism in this period for the modern person to comprehend is the practice of ritual purity. The basis of the rules on purity is rooted in the Torah but were later expanded and codified by later generations. In the first century though, purity was widely practiced judging by the numerous emersion pools that have been found dotted around the modern nation of Israel.

Impurity could be contracted and spread through a number of different ways; male ejaculation and female menstruation were but two common ways of becoming impure. Contact with a sufferer of leprosy (which in the ancient times included everything from acne to eczema) was another way, and the impurity could even be received through contact with a leper's clothes or by simply being in his home. Being in a state of impurity meant that the person could not approach the Temple to offer sacrifices, but fortunately there were instructions on how one could become pure again. Invariably this meant a splash of water followed by a wait of a few days and then one would be pure. Purity laws were necessarily more stringent for the clan of the priests since these men served the Temple, and as the Temple was the dwelling place of God on earth they had to be free of impurity.

Another important aspect of Judaism in this era was the Temple centered in Jerusalem. As we saw earlier, some Jews were prepared to fight to maintain the sanctity of the Temple and keep it free from pagan influence and idols. Jesus would have lived during the second Temple period and when he visited it was most likely still under construction. It was at the Temple that sacrifices of grain and animals were made to the almighty God. If one had somehow contravened one of God's commandments a Jew could offer up a sacrifice at the Temple as a means to ensure atonement for their sin. Once the correct sacrifice was given (the Torah specified exactly what sacrifice was required for what sin) and the correct rituals were observed the Jew was once again free of sin, but of course it was much better to avoid sinning in the first place.

On special holidays, the Temple mount would have been heaving with thousands of pilgrims. Passover, the festival at which Jesus would eventually meet his fate, was a particularly busy and chaotic time as pilgrims from all the Jewish provinces and from all over the Diaspora would assemble with their animal offerings. A male member of the family would be selected to take the offering to the Temple, which would mean he would have to undergo a special purification ritual before he could enter. Only a priest could slaughter the offering, he would cut the creature's throat to drain the blood and then parts of the carcass were burned at the altar. The priest would take a share of the meat and the remaining portions would be taken back to the family to be consumed. To say that the Passover festival would be a chaotic affront to the senses, what with all the incense, dung, blood and burning entrails, is an understatement.

Although the Temple represented the central institution of Judaism in this period, in practice those Jews living in the Diaspora would be unlikely to attend all of the festivals. They did voluntarily collect their special annual tax and send it to the Temple as was required of all law abiding Jews no matter where they lived. The Roman authorities even protected these monies from those who might have been tempted to dip their hands into the pot. Thus, despite being geographically far from the Temple the Diaspora Jews remained close to it in heart and continued to remember its importance to their religion. Instead the Diaspora Jews attended the synagogues present in large urban areas where they would read aloud the Torah and interpret its laws. No sacrifices were conducted at the synagogue because only at the Temple could they be offered. The Temple remained firmly burned on the mind of all Jews as the central and most important location of their faith and certainly the most zealous among them in the past had been prepared to die when they thought the Temple was being polluted by foreign influence.

The most intriguing aspect of first century Judaism that has direct implications for the study of Jesus is that many Jews of the second temple era were expecting a messiah to be sent from God. Ever since the destruction of the first Temple at the hands of the Babylonians, and the Jewish people's exile, there had been an increasing yearning for an anointed one (in Greek this anointment is called Christos), one especially chosen by God, one who like the great King David would usher in a new dawn of peace in a united Israel. In the first instances of this expectation they hoped only for a nationalistic/military leader who could cast aside the bonds of injustice that they felt under the Babylonians. Yet this expectation had evolved somewhat so that by Jesus' time some Jews thought that the messiah would bring with him angelic armies to fight against the forces of evil. After the Maccabean revolt there was an additional idea that the dead would be physically raised from their graves and all of this became associated with the coming messiah. It is difficult to gauge how prevalent this idea was, perhaps it was not at all universal, but a good proportion of Jews were expecting the messiah to come and renew the kingdom of Israel.

By all accounts, the Jews expected the messiah to be a mortal man. There is no precedent for a divine messiah in any of the old prophecies. At any rate, the messianic age was generally understood to be a time of peace when all foreign nations would look to Israel for guidance and would beg forgiveness for past transgressions against her. They would look to the Jews as spiritual leaders and all would worship the one true God – the God of the Israelites. In this divine era the Jews themselves would know the Torah without having to study it and because of their closeness with God they would find joy and gladness for the rest of time. This messianic age is sometimes known as the 'Kingdom of God' and is predicted in the book of Isaiah in the Old Testament.

Variations of these themes were evidently in existence at the time of Jesus. From the texts of the Dead Sea Scrolls we know that the community at Qumran was expecting a type of dual messiahship, a priestly messiah and a kingly one. Biblical Scholar Robert Eisman comments that these two messiahs were later blended together. What is clear, however, is that the Qumran community, living shortly before Jesus' career, expected an earth shattering event that would eventually lead to the redemption of Israel.

Religious Tension Under The Romans

The Romans have been condemned by history for throwing Christians to the lions, but far from being anti-religious they were always in favor of keeping the local gods happy. As a general rule, communities administered by the Romans were free to worship their own deities in any way they liked as long as it didn't interfere with taxes and didn't interfere with the peace. Often it was the case that the Romans took onboard local deities, for example the cult of Isis originating in

Egypt was widespread in the Empire and was practiced by many of her citizens. There were plenty of gods and they all deserved reverence and sacrifice. Furthermore, it was quite acceptable for a citizen to be a participant of multiple cults. Effectively, they were free to pick and choose which cults and customs appealed to them. To the Roman mind, the Jewish practice of rejecting all gods except one was strange, rude even.

Although the Romans had tolerated Jews within the Empire, their special religion must have seemed strange compared to their own polytheistic religions. When Pompey had crushed resistance in his siege of Jerusalem there was no one to stop him entering the holiest place in the Jewish Temple. The holy of holies within the Temple was the most sacred point of all Israel, it was where God himself resided, and no one except the high priest was ever allowed inside and even he would enter but once a year after much ritual and preparation. What did the conquering Pompey find when he entered? The residence of a living god? No. Apart from some curtains there was nothing – not even a statue of the deity which was most perplexing to his religious sensibilities.

Indeed, throughout the history of Roman rule in Judea we see continuous infringements on Jewish ideals by the foreign pagans who simply could not understand the intricacies of Jewish monotheism and its disgust at worshipping images of gods carved into stone.

That is not to say that the Romans were completely against the Jewish religion. Far from it. They had always held the ancient Jewish scriptures in awe. Anything that old must be important. In fact, many imperials had been drawn to Judaism precisely because of its venerable age and ancient traditions.

Despite centuries of foreign rule, the Jews had still held onto their most powerful beliefs, including a strict prohibition of worshipping idols. This was the law as explicitly commanded to the Jewish people by God through his prophet Moses. Idolatry was considered one of the worse transgressions. The book of Deuteronomy 6:5 makes this clear:

"And thou shall love the Lord thy God with all thy heart, and with all thy soul, and with all thy might."

And it would be better to kill yourself than to break this law by worshipping any other divinity other than God. With this in mind, it is much easier to understand why the Jews were ready to fight and die to protect the holy Temple from pagan influence and golden eagles. God himself commanded absolute obedience from his special people. To worship an idol was to ignore God's will.

The unique differences between Roman and Jewish religious practice coupled with the Roman inability to grasp the essential points of Judaism, especially regarding idolatry, led to conflicts in Judea. This had happened before when the Greeks tried to Hellenize the Temple, and it was going to happen again. The slightest form of idolatry could inflame the Jews, even the standards carried by the Roman legions were idols since they served as portable shrines for the troops and their presence in the holy land infuriated the Jews. The greatest affront, however, was over Emperor Caligula's attempt to install a statue of himself in the Temple. Caligula (12 – 41 CE) was offended that the Jews refused to offer the proper veneration to himself, a living deity, and was prepared to fight them over it. The Jews too were set for death rather than idols but fortunately for them Caligula was murdered before things got out of hand.

Josephus tells us that years later it is the Greeks sacrificing birds outside of a Jewish synagogue in the city of Caesarea that sparked the violence that erupted into the First Jewish War (66-60 CE). Though this may be an oversimplification, since taxation was also added to the list of grievances by the rebels, it is evident that some sections of Jewish society were prepared to use their religion as a rallying point of rebellion and were ready to die to uphold God's commandments.

During this war, at one point it seemed that the rebels might actually succeed in defeating the Romans. A band of Jewish rebels had managed to ambush and defeat an entire Roman legion in the Battle of Beth Horon in 66 CE. As it was, the legions would return in greater numbers to wreak a terrible vengeance, which culminated in the siege of Jerusalem and the destruction of Herod's Temple in 70 CE

Another revolt many years later (the Bar Kokha revolt 132–136 CE) was to be the last and most decisive Jewish uprising. Here the Emperor Hadrian had promised the Jews that he would rebuild Jerusalem and there was hope among the people that under his leadership there would be peace. But there upon the ruins of the Temple sprang a pagan temple dedicated to Jupiter, thus adding insult to injury. After a visit to Jerusalem, Hadrian decided instead that the city would make an excellent place to base the legions, but what really incensed the natives was his declaration that Jews should never be permitted to enter the city. This was too much for the Jews to handle and war prevailed.

The chief leader of this revolt was Simeon Bar Kokhba. He managed to inflict heavy losses on the Roman enemy and among his followers rumors were brewing that Bar Kokhba might just be the messiah who would re-unite Israel under one king. It was not to be. Rome was too powerful. After three long years Bar Kokhba was defeated and in disgust the Emperor wiped Israel from the map, instead branding these lands as Syria

Palestine, a final insult to the Jews by naming their nation after their ancient enemies - the Philistines.

Political and Religious Sects in The Age of Jesus

The chief instigators of violence in the Jewish uprisings, according to Josephus, were the Zealots. The zealots are violently opposed to foreign rule from the first moment that the Romans step foot in Judea. They perpetrate violence and murder against non-Jews and plot war. Josephus tells us that this movement first arose under Judah the Galilean, who opposed the Census of Quirnus (6 or 7 CE the census was a Roman survey of its provinces in Syria and Judea for tax collection) with disastrous results. In the Talmud (a collection of ancient rabbinic writings on Jewish law and traditionally written circa 200 CE) the Zealots come across as a violent bunch of men who in the face of certain failure would not compromise to save the survivors in the besieged Temple in the First Jewish War. Josephus' depiction of them has them lording over a reign of terror on the Jewish lands.

Perhaps worse were the Sicarii – the dagger men, who not only opposed the Gentiles, but were willing to target and assassinate Jews seen to be collaborating with the Romans. Both the Zealots and the Sicarii would remain a thorn in the side of the Romans until they are eventually defeated in the Bar Kokhba revolt.

Part of their violent attitude might derive from their hatred of being ruled by foreigners but these men are not mere freedom fighters. There was a worse fate than being crucified by the Romans, there was the wrath of God. Therefore, although these groups had a very political agenda they were also motivated by religion. Religion and politics in this time were indistinguishable.

Later generation of Jews who had survived these turbulent times would largely blame the Zealots for bringing about the destruction of the Temple because of their stubborn commitment to violence. Yet these groups do present an interesting angle on the Jesus story because we read in the New Testament that among Jesus' closest followers, the twelve disciples, there is Judas Iscariot (Sicarii) and Simeon the Zealot. An assassin and a revolutionary in Jesus' most trusted circle? This has led to some scholars to reconstruct the mission of Jesus as a kind of political struggle against the Romans.

Aside from these violent agitators, Josephus described three distinct political and religious factions in Israel of this period. These groups disagreed amongst themselves over everything from the interpretation of the law to the correct methods of ritual purity and they professed differing sets of beliefs. The three groups specified by Josephus are the Sadducees, the Pharisees and the Essenes.

At the top end of the Jewish spectrum we have those of the ruling classes who are desperate to both keep the Roman overlords happy and suppress the rebels. The Sadducees are associated with the day-to-day running of the Temple including sacrificing and burning the animals, but have often been viewed as the 'priest-kings' of the age. They represent the higher echelons of Jewish society, the religious conservatives, and from among their number the high priest was selected. This was a political as well as a religious position and one that was carefully administered by the Romans. The Sadducees also had their own set of beliefs; Josephus tells us that they did not believe in the immortality of the soul nor a punishment/reward scheme in the afterlife. The Sadducees as the ruling elite, needless to say, had plenty of enemies among the common Jews; the Zealots saw them as collaborators with the enemy, and another sect, the Pharisees opposed them for their differences in belief.

The Pharisees were from the 'working class' of Israel at this time and as such did not have any control over the Temple or what went on there. They disliked that the Sadducees were becoming more and more Hellenized and so the Pharisees stuck rigidly to their own interpretation of the law that was less focused on the Temple. Instead, the Pharisees extended the Mosaic Law to the home, making worship a more democratic practice. Such mundane activity as the correct way to clean a plate was one aspect of the philosophy but generally speaking they seem to be concerned with a commitment to social justice. Great leaders were not born into the position, as were the Sadducees, but could come about through scholarly achievement.

Both of these groups are of interest to students of the historical Jesus because the gospels have Jesus standing trial at the Sanhedrin (similar to a court of law) which was largely overseen by the Sadducees and Jesus also criticizes the Pharisees for their overreliance on the mundane aspects of law keeping. But there is another group worth mentioning here, that of the Essenes of whom the community at Qumran, the originators of the Dead Sea Scrolls, have been identified with.

The Essenes rejected earthly wealth to live an ascetic lifestyle in the cities and deserts of Israel. This was not a united group (if any of the Jewish groups were ever united) and they practiced a wide range of philosophies for the worship of God. They were variably mystic and messianic. The Jewish philosopher Philo (20 – 50 CE) paints a portrait of the Essenes living together and sharing everything between each other. They eschewed voluntary poverty, and shared their food and clothes amongst each other. As marriage was considered an earthly pleasure, they rejected this too. Josephus tells us that the Essenes ritually immersed themselves often and devoted themselves to charity. He says they avoided the expression of anger, avoided oaths, and avoided animal sacrifice. Because of their communal living many have been tempted to see them in a similar light to monks in the medieval period of Christianity and others have seen elements of their teaching in Jesus' own words.

There were many diverse Jewish groups of the period with complicated relationships between each other. Above is a mere summary of them. Although they did not always get along with each other, they were still 'united' in considering themselves to be Jews – they believed in one God and believed Moses had given them the law.

The Galileans

To illustrate some of the differences among the Jews of this period, we shall now examine what it meant to be a Galilean, which will also help us to build a picture of Jesus as a historical person because Jesus was born in a small village in the Galilee. The ancients did seem to hold certain prejudices and stereotypes of the average Galilean and likely applied these to the figure of Jesus when he arrived in Judea to attend the Passover festival shortly before his demise.

From 4 BCE – 39 CE the Galilee had been ruled by Herod Antipas (one son who escaped his father Herod the Great's murderous rule) and while Judea was coming under heavy Roman influence after being incorporated into the Empire, the Galilee had for a short time remained independent. Though little is known about the administration of this province it is known that Antipas had his own tax collectors and it is likely that he had his own rules that differed from the better known system established in Judea.

By all indications the Galilee was a rich and fertile region. There were plenty of small settlements in between larger towns, which made a living from working the land and from fishing in the Sea of Galilee. The province, with its abundant agriculture, was self sufficient and even had enough to export for profit. Galilean olive oil found its way to tables across the Roman Empire.

Despite being a land of farmers and fishermen, the Galileans were not without their wealth. Perhaps an indication of this is given in the gospels themselves when we learn that the fishermen on the lake had hired additional hands to assist with their work[4]. This suggests a business-like operation rather than individual fishermen seeking to feed their families.

This vision of a wealthy independent region is one thing, but Galileans were renowned for being troublemakers. During the reign of Emperor Augustus, the Romans incorporated the Jewish regions of Judea, Samaria and Idumea into the province of Syria. The governor of Syria, Publius Sulpicius Quirinius, ordered a census of these new lands for the purpose of collecting tax in 6 CE. Josephus tells us that the zealots were opposed to paying any tax to the Romans and rose up in revolt. As we saw earlier, at the head of violent opposing was Judas the Galilean. Additionally, during the uprising the Judeans were ready to accept terms with the Romans, recognizing that defeat was inevitable. Yet it was the Galileans who were prepared to fight to the death for their beliefs and urged their

---

[4] Mark 1:20

countrymen to continue the fight. In both cases the Galileans were at the center of the trouble.

It wasn't only the Romans who might have seen Galileans as troublemakers. Later rabbinic texts, such as the Misnah, record the Galileans being an aggressive people who were happy to squabble amongst themselves. These were a rough and sturdy breed of farmers and workers who would have been easily distinguishable from their more sophisticated Judean cousins by their rough pronunciation of Aramaic. An incident is preserved in the Talmud of a Galilean being ridiculed in the Jerusalem market for his rough accent:

> *"You stupid Galilean, do you want something to ride on [hamar: a donkey]? Or something to drink [hamar: wine]? Or something for a sacrifice [immar: a lamb]?"*[5]

Even in our times city types are known to poke fun of the country yokels and the same was happening back then. Another incident in the gospels supports this. A servant girl asks Peter whether he was with the group of Jesus' followers, saying *"Surely you are one of them, for your accent gives you away."*[6]

Galileans appeared to be less strict in their observance of ritual purity. Indeed, one Yochanan ben Zakai, a Pharisaic Jewish sage complains that during all his years in the Galilee he was only asked twice about the Jewish law, causing him to practically cry in despair.[7] Later, Jesus will likewise criticize the Pharisee's overreliance on observing the more mundane aspects of the law.

That the Christians would proclaim Jesus of Nazareth, a mere Galilean, as messiah was perhaps understandably lamented, as this incident in the gospel's show:

---

[5] Mishnah Erubin 53b
[6] Matthew 26:73
[7] Mishnah Shabbat 15d

"Nazareth! Can anything good come from there?" cries Nathaniel in the gospel of John.[8] The messiah was meant to be a kingly character and not a simple peasant from the backwaters of Israel with a gruff accent.

The Galileans had remained distinct from their Judean cousins, but not as far gone as the Samaritans. The Samaritans considered themselves to be Jews but the fact that their version of the Torah differed somewhat from other versions meant that there was tension between them. The Samaritans claimed that their Torah was the true version; the one that hadn't been corrupted over time when the Judeans had been exiled by the Babylonians. In their version of things, it is the Mount Gerizim in their lands in which Yahweh had ordered a great temple to be built, and not the Temple mount in Jerusalem. Judeans were to destroy the Samaritan temple sometime in the second century BCE. Interestingly, this prejudice against the Samaritans survived into Christian times, and the Christian Romans barred them from worshipping at their mountain.

Perhaps the most important region in this time, however, was Judea. This is where most of the events of history played out. It is here that the one 'true' Temple is located and it is to this Temple that the pilgrims from Galilee would come; crossing the dangerous Samaritan lands to arrive there. And it is in Judea where Jesus would be strung up and executed. Judea was where all the groups mentioned by Josephus would come head to head; with the Sadducees ruling the Temple and below them the Pharisees criticizing them and the zealots plotting to violently overthrow the traditional order. Eventually, Jesus, a rough sounding peasant from the Galilee would enter this powder keg.

---

[8] John 1:46

Charismatic Holy Men

Wandering these lands were all kinds of revolutionaries, assassins and bandits but there seems to be another minority of people who are especially important to the discovery of a historical Jesus. There were certain Jewish holy men who attracted popular followings among the people because of their unique messages and appeal to the scriptures. Some supposedly could also perform miracles. Special as Jesus may seem, if anything he seems to fit quite snugly into what might be termed the archetypal charismatic healer and wonder worker of who we shall now meet several more.

John the Baptist is best known to us from the gospels as the man who baptized Jesus. Recall the role of water in ritual purity, well John was essentially purifying people of their sins by dipping them in the running water of the River Jordan. He was immensely popular in these times, although not with the ruling classes but with the ordinary people.

John's followers would continue even after John's death and some of them would be encountered in the Book of Acts, which records the early church's attempts to convert the Gentiles of the wider Empire. There is one Apollo from Alexandria in modern day Egypt who is a preacher but who had known only the baptism of John[9]. John's influence must have been great indeed if his teaching was known so far away.

However, popularity with the people was dangerous to the authorities. Scholars have indicated that this might be the reason for why John was executed. Josephus supports this, he tells us that:

> *"Herod, who feared lest the great influence John had over the people might put it into his power and inclination to*

---

[9] Acts 18:25

raise a rebellion, (for they seemed ready to do anything
he should advise) thought it best, by putting him to
death, to prevent any mischief he might cause."[10]

Later on, when Herod's army is routed in battle many Jews understood this as a sign that God was angry over Herod's execution of this holy man.

The baptizer is a wild sort of character, living in a cave and feeding off honey and locusts (no fear of impurity in that diet). He preaches to those who turn up and cleanses them of sin in the river Jordon. If we are to believe the gospel of Luke, then John the Baptist, like Jesus, is born through a miracle. The angel Gabriel forewarns his aged mother that her child will be great in the eyes of God and despite having been sterile she gives birth to John.

John of the gospels is born as a kind of precursor to the coming of Jesus and the gospels frame his story in the light of the coming messianic age. While preaching from the banks of the Jordan, the baptizer is looking upwards expectantly and awaiting the coming of a new age of justice and righteousness, like many Jews of his age must have done. At least this is what the gospels tell us. Clearly, John was an important man of his time, so important in fact that he is re-invented by the gospels to be incorporated into Jesus' story.

John must be seen from the perspective of the first century Jew. He wasn't only baptizing people in a river; he was doing it in the River Jordan, which is the scene of several miracles in the Old Testament. When the Jews carrying the Ark of the Covenant reach the river the water stops flowing allowing them to pass with ease, a story that echoes Moses parting of the seas. The revered

---

[10] Antiquities 18.5.2

Prophets Elijah and Elisha both would cross the river and Elisha performs a miraculous healing there.

Indeed, there appeared numerous popular wonder workers whose actions mirrored the great prophets of the past. In the Jewish Antiquities, Josephus tells us that:

> "...while Fadus was procurator of Judea, a certain charlatan, whose name was Theudas, persuaded a great part of the people to take their effects with them, and follow him to the river Jordan; for he told them he was a prophet, and that he would, by his own command, divide the river, and afford them an easy passage over it. Many were deluded by his words. However, Fadus did not permit them to make any advantage of his wild attempt, but sent a troop of horsemen out against them. After falling upon them unexpectedly, they slew many of them, and took many of them alive. They also took Theudas alive, cut off his head, and carried it to Jerusalem."[11]

This episode is interesting because we see a charismatic, religious leader attracting a substantial crowd based on a promise that he would perform some miracle inspired from scripture. In this case, dividing the river is an allusion to Joshua in the Old Testament where the river stops flowing to allow the Ark of the Covenant to pass safely.[12] Since the original story is connected with the redemption of Israel perhaps this Thuedas thought of himself as the Jewish messiah. But once again we see the authorities discomfort with large assemblages of crowds and the Roman procurator sends out the cavalry to disperse them and Theudas himself is executed in 46 CE.

Here is another example from Josephus of an incident dating to around 52-58 CE.

---

[11] Antiquities 20.5.1
[12] Joshua 3.14-17

"...About this time, someone came out of Egypt to Jerusalem, claiming to be a prophet. He advised the crowd to go along with him to the Mount of Olives, as it was called, which lay over against the city, and at the distance of a kilometer. He added that he would show them from hence how the walls of Jerusalem would fall down at his command, and he promised them that he would procure them an entrance into the city through those collapsed walls. Now when Felix was informed of these things, he ordered his soldiers to take their weapons, and came against them with a great number of horsemen and footmen from Jerusalem, and attacked the Egyptian and the people that were with him. He slew four hundred of them, and took two hundred alive. The Egyptian himself escaped out of the fight, but did not appear anymore."[13]

Again, the Egyptian was inspired by events in scripture, in particular Joshua 6.20 and the destruction of the walls of Jericho. The Mount of Olives is also important since in Zechariah 14.4 this is where God will stand in judgment. By promising miracles in significant locations we might deduce that these types of men were alluding to the scriptures and possibly harbored messianic expectations. What is obvious, however, is charismatic holy men were present in our era and their messages found a willing audience. John, Theudas and the Egyptian all attracted large crowds. The ruling authorities, because of the threat of rebellion, were rather wary of these types of men and were willing to kill them and their followers to preserve the peace. But these examples serve to show us the religious fervor of the age. Men came, promising miracles, attracted large crowds and ultimately were killed by the authorities.

---

[13] Jewish War 20.13.5

Another man who promised miracles and attracted crowds was Jesus and he too will die at the hands of the Romans.

Conclusions

Although the history of Israel and its religion is complicated, here we have sketched a brief outline that will allow us to understand a little more about Jesus and how he came to be regarded first as messiah and then as a God. Of particular interest, it must be noted, that although the Jews were prone to disagree amongst themselves they did have certain things in common. They believed that there was one God. This God could send foreign armies to punish or reward the Jews just as he could punish individuals with sickness or reward them with long, healthy lives. There was also a widely held belief that God worked through his prophets, the most important of whom was Moses. Moses and his laws were still observed in Jesus' time although there always was room for interpretation.

Among the prophecies in the scriptures was an idea that God had promised that a descendent of King David would reunite Israel and the twelve tribes. By the time of Jesus there were many expecting a messiah figure to arrive and usher in a Kingdom of God where justice would prevail and where the Gentiles would turn to the God of Israel. This is best evidenced in the Dead Sea Scrolls.

During Roman rule in Judea, there were many cultural misunderstandings, especially when the Romans seemed oblivious to the intricacies of Judaism. The Romans ruled alongside the Sadducees who maintained the Temple and favored a traditional interpretation of the law. Some of the population however resented foreign rule, especially after Herod had removed the Hasmonean dynasty. Revolt was on the horizon.

Amid the different sects were a variety of charismatic teachers and wonder workers who are unanimously killed because their popularity. Religion of this period was often synonymous with politics. One such example was Simon Bar Kokhba who was proclaimed messiah by his supporters in the hope he would reunite Israel. The Romans had no moral qualms with executing troublemakers and they would have been extremely wary of men who used such political terms as the 'Kingdom of God'. Equally, they had no issues with executing popular leaders.

It is amid this chaotic scene that Jesus is born. Like many of this period, Jesus came promising miracles but additionally he preached the Kingdom of God. Years after his crucifixion, stories of his life remained in circulation until they were eventually written down in the gospels. To further understand Jesus we must understand the gospels.

CHAPTER TWO

Bias of the Biographers

It may seem strange for a skeptical portrait of Jesus to rely on the gospels as a source of historical information but practically everything we know about Jesus' life is handed to us through them. The gospels simply cannot be ignored because they represent the major source of information about Jesus. The critical historian must then deal with them as they would with any source from antiquity and evaluate their usefulness by understanding who wrote them, why and when.

At a first glance, the gospels appear to represent historical accounts. They are filled with specific details, such as names, times, places and events that are occurring within the timeframe of first century Israel. This lends a certain authority to them because we can check this data against other ancient sources to determine their reliability. The temptation for Christians is to assume that since there are some historical aspects within the texts then everything else must be accurate. Indeed, Christians ancient and modern have assumed that the gospels represent an accurate truth written by authors who were very close, or even eye witness, to the events that are portrayed.

Modern Evangelical works such as Lee Strobel's '*A Case for Christ*' for example, invite the reader to assemble all of the available information concerning Jesus and evaluate them, much in the same way that a journalist or even a court of law would do. Strobel then argues that we can trust the gospels. He says that the gospels are an excellent source of information for the life of Jesus because they are early and did not have time to be corrupted. Inconsistencies between the four accounts do not cause a problem for Strobel either. The argument goes that every respective eyewitness will see things differently and this is why there are certain errors in the version of events. In the end, his point is that it is much more valuable to have four distinct witnesses rather than just one, so the gospels are a great way for us to know about Jesus. Presumably, once we have accepted the gospels as, well, 'gospel truth', then we can accept that Jesus was the Son of God who came to wash away our sins.

The gospels tell us that Jesus was able to perform miracles, healings and that he could exorcise demons. These are invariable seen as signs of his true power - this was the messiah, this was the Son of God. Jesus was the eternal logos, the word of God, who had existed from the beginning of time. We must trust in him to achieve an afterlife. What then if we can demonstrate the gospels to be flawed, inaccurate and biased?

In this chapter we shall examine the four canonical gospels in the New Testament in much the same way as Strobel proposes, although as we shall see, the conclusions of the secular historian are vastly different from those of an evangelical Christian. In the end the gospels are much like any source that has survived through the ages; they too are subject to bias and were written for specific reasons. The inconsistencies in them do not strengthen the case for Jesus, but in places are so fundamentally opposed to each other that we must wonder which version is correct, if any of them are.

What is a Gospel?

Before we begin dismissing the claims of the evangelists it is prudent to first examine what actually we mean when we talk about a gospel. The term gospel is derived from the Greek word 'evangelion' which literally means good tidings, or good news. Translated into Old English this becomes 'God Spell' which has evolved into the modern term 'Gospel'.

The genre of the gospel is unique to Christianity, being a kind of biographical narrative centered historically on the times and locations of Jesus' life. The four gospels in the New Testament paint a picture of Jesus by focusing on his public career, his preaching and the miracles that he performed. They are filled with stories from his life, the people he met, taught and healed, the places he visited and the deeds he performed. There is also a great emphasis on the final moments of his life leading up to his execution, indeed this is the main point of the story. Jesus lived only so that he could die. From Jesus' portrayal in the gospels it is easier to assume that they were written for theological reasons – that is they were written to express a religious point about who Jesus was. Critical historians universally adhere to this view.

The four gospels canonized in the New Testament are not the only gospels in existence. In ancient times there were actually very many gospels floating around and each one had its own unique twist to the Jesus story. One of the most famous, or if you prefer, more notorious is the Gospel of Judas, which has courted controversy in recent years and has been the subject of much debate. In this version Judas betrays Jesus because it was part of the plan. Judas betrays his master out of humility to him, and therefore is not such a bad guy after all. The existence of this gospel is interesting, not because it can shed light on what actually transpired between Jesus and his disciple, the gospel of Judas is too late for that, but because it shows us that there were many other interpretations about the life of Jesus in early Christianity. Many alternative gospels were written, in fact we have ten complete gospels in existence and scores of fragmented ones. Some gospels were mentioned by early writers but are now lost to us but only four made it into the bible. These alternative gospels are known as the Apocrypha (which means 'hidden'). Many apocryphal gospels were rejected by the emerging Catholic Church on the grounds that they were late or did not conform to the teachings of the church. Indeed, Judas appears to have been composed sometime in the mid second century and certainly its teachings do not conform to the dominant forms of Christianity of that age.

The Gospel of Judas like most of the apocryphal works was not a deliberate attempt to deceive the believers away from mainstream beliefs. Whoever wrote them evidently believed in the version of events that they described and the hidden gospels were held in high regard among the communities that created and revered them. It should be remembered that these early Christians did not have an established and 'authentic' bible as we have today. They didn't even have an accepted set of beliefs. Some of the earliest Christians for example believed Jesus to be a mere man with a physical body while others held him to be a divinity with a spiritual presence. The differences were numerous and led to the creation of a multitude of alternative gospels to reflect these diverse beliefs.

The four gospels of the New Testament became to be favored above all others around 185 CE when Irenaeus of Lyons, an early church father, denounced other sects of Christianity for using only one gospel each or using newer gospels. He favored the four precisely because they were early but also because they enjoyed widespread popularity in the Empire of his day. Despite Irenaeus' arguments for using the four gospels it wasn't until 382 CE that the western Orthodox Church met at the Council of Rome to accept our current biblical format (known as the canon) which included the four gospels. Alternative gospels were deemed heretical or too late to be genuine and were therefore rejected and did not make it into the bible. Despite this many apocryphal works were still copied and studied until quite late. Certainly, Geoffrey Chaucer was familiar with some of the apocrypha when he was composing the Canterbury Tales. For example, during the Miller's Tale he mentions the Harrowing of Hell which is a story of Jesus entering hell that was contained originally in the Gospel of Nicodemus composed circa 350 CE. This demonstrates that long after they were rejected the Apocrypha continued to be popular and exert an influence on the western mind.

Who Wrote The Gospels?

Traditionally, the four gospels are said to have been written by Mark, Matthew, Luke and John. These men are invariably held to be original followers of Jesus or at least followers of the original disciples, except in the case of Luke where he is said to be a follower of Paul – an early Christian who spent most of his time in the Roman Empire converting people.

These ascriptions to authorship however come to us from the writings of the church fathers later on in the second century CE. According to the church father Papias (possibly living in the period 60-135 CE and quoted by the later Eusebius who lived circa 263-339 CE), the gospel of Mark was written down by a student of one of Jesus' original disciples, and he did record this teaching accurately. Papias likely recorded what was commonly believed about the origin of the gospel, but this is hearsay and we have to be very careful indeed if we are to assume he is correct. The earliest surviving gospels written on papyrus scrolls do not contain punctuation, headings, numberings and are without names. Essentially, the gospels are anonymous.

Another obstacle in proclaiming Mark to be the author of this gospel is the fact that there were many forgeries circulating in ancient times. We know that certain, later gospels, were indeed written by an anonymous author in the name of someone else. Sometimes these forgeries were written by followers of a certain teacher in what was essentially an act of humility. The student recognized that the master was the superior mind and would then attribute his own work to him. At other times fakes came into existence when someone had something really important to say but lacked the name and fame to be listened to. By writing a text in the name of a famous person their ideas were more likely to be read and circulated. Sometimes, profit was a good motivation for faking another's work.

Forgeries were a constant irritation to some of the ancient minds, for example Galen, the famous Roman physician, who got so annoyed that others were publishing works under his name that he wrote a book called 'on his own books' that would help his readers to authenticate his genuine works. Bearing in mind that forgery was evidently prevalent in the ancient world we must therefore be very careful indeed in ascribing authors to any of the gospels. Other texts in the New Testament are known to be forgeries. Paul was also a victim of ancient forgers. From his thirteen letters (known as Epistles) within the New Testament, scholars can only agree that seven of them are genuine. Paul's Epistle to the Hebrews is one example unanimously understood by scholars to be a fake. Whoever wrote this epistle wanted to get their point across and used Paul's name to do so.

It would be nice if we did have an accurate first hand report by an eye witness to the life of Jesus but there is simply no evidence to show that the gospels are anything like this. Bearing in mind the pervasiveness of forgeries and the shaky evidence we have for naming the authors of each of the gospels, it is safer to simply assume that they are all anonymous. That does not mean that we cannot scour them for information because whoever did write them likely inherited some earlier information and used this as a basis for their compositions.

When Were The Gospels Written?

Dating the gospels is notoriously difficult and the debate over which gospel is the earliest continues. Solid arguments have given priority to each gospel at one time or another but these days the common consensus is that Mark is the earliest, likely written sometime between 65-70 CE, at least forty years after Jesus was executed. The Gospel of Matthew is tailored for a Jewish audience and has been dated to around 80-85 CE. Luke is a companion piece with the Book of Acts and is regarded as the most artistic of the gospels and was likely written 85-90 CE. The very latest is commonly assumed to be the Gospel of John, dated 90-110 CE

The prime reason why Mark is dated first is because his version of Jesus is considerably less developed than the others. Mark's Jesus is a man, albeit one with an important mission and the ability to heal, and he is very secretive about his true identity. On the other hand, John's version describes Jesus as the everlasting 'logos' who has been in existence since the beginning of time and his character has no qualms about proclaiming his divine background to anyone. This method of dating supposes that the more legendary material that has formed then the later the text is. John with his highly developed divine Jesus is therefore later than Mark's more primitive and more human Jesus.

Actually, the gospels do represent a very early source of information about the life of Jesus. In the case of Mark, several decades had passed since the death of Jesus and the composition of his gospel. This is actually a very small amount of time when we consider that the earliest sources dealing with Alexander the Great are written centuries after his death. This does not mean however that the gospels are more accurate, since as we shall shortly demonstrate, they were written by believers and were written for theological reasons.

Like any historical source, we can read through the gospels and look for events that appear out of place from the original context and use them to date the text. Thus when Jesus predicts that not a stone will be left unturned on the Temple in Jerusalem, we know that during his own lifetime the temple was still being built, but that in 70 CE the Roman army destroyed the Temple during the First Jewish War. From a religious perspective, it can be said that Jesus has just made a prophecy that came true, but to the skeptic it seems the gospel writers had the advantage of hindsight when they were compiling their work.

Chapter thirteen of the gospel of Mark and the parallel passages in Matthew and Luke, which contains the vision of a destroyed temple, is known as the 'little apocalypse'. The events described here seem out of place from the preceding text, as if someone pasted it in later over the original. After Jesus has described how the Temple would be destroyed, several of his disciples ask him privately when these events would happen. Jesus then describes a series of calamities, including wars and rumors of wars. Nation will rise up against nation, and kingdom against kingdom and those in Judea will flee to the mountains. It has often been argued that this passage was influenced by events of the First Jewish War which culminated in the destruction of the Temple.

In the same chapter we have other predictions, *"You will be handed over to the local councils and flogged in the synagogues,"* and *"All men will hate you because of me."* These statements seem to reflect the first persecutions against Christians that were occurring during the time when Mark thirteen was being written. From the Book of Acts we do see Paul taking a beating and standing in front of local councils which sound very similar to what Mark is describing. Therefore, we can say with some certainty that events occurring after Jesus' death had an impact on the composition of the gospels, which helps us to date them accordingly.

How Were The Gospels Written?

It is a mistake to assume that since there are four early gospels in the bible that we have four unique sources of information about Jesus; this is a common argument among present day evangelists. Only 3% of the material in Mark is unique to that gospel. The remaining 97% has been copied by Luke and Matthew and in some places there has been a word-for-word transcription. In fact, if the three works of Mark, Matthew and Luke are placed together there are amazing similarities both in content, character and chronology which is why these three gospels are called the synoptic gospels (synoptic is Greek for 'seen together').

That Matthew and Luke based their accounts on Mark is another line of evidence for placing Mark as the earliest of the gospels. It is highly likely that Luke and Matthew had a copy of the first gospel in their hands when they were composing their own works. When the synoptics are read alongside each other it becomes quite clear that the bare bones of Marks work were fleshed out in Luke and Matthew- their gospels are longer, meatier but still rely on Mark's timeline.

Both Matthew and Luke also shared another source in common which the writer of Mark did not have. Both of these gospels share approximately a quarter of their material with each other but this material is absent from Mark. Historians have speculated that there must have been another source in circulation which Luke and Matthew incorporated into their gospels but which is now lost to us. By comparing the similarities between these two gospels, scholars are able to reconstruct what this source looked like. This is the hypothetical Q source (from Quelle meaning 'source' in German) which scholars since the nineteenth century have speculated on.

Since the shared content in Matthew and Luke are mostly spoken words of Jesus, the reconstructed Q document looks like a simple list of all the sayings of Jesus minus the narrative framework (which they pinched from Mark). It would be as if one had compiled a list of Winston Churchill quotations but neglected to mention when and where he was when he said them. So a later Churchill biographer might use the line 'we will fight them on the bridges' to describe the leader's experience fighting in the Sudan as a young officer instead of during his time as Prime Minister in the Second World War.

Luke and Matthew apparently cut and pasted content from Q into their own narratives. The same sayings appear in these gospels but each in different places of the narrative. As an example, the gospel of Matthew has Jesus teaching in the Temple courts when he is approached by the chief priest who challenges his authority. Jesus then launches himself into a long speech containing the parable of the wedding banquet.

In Luke's gospel this same parable, although slightly altered, appears when Jesus is sitting around the house of a Pharisee. The parables are the same but are put into different contexts in the narrative, which suggests that originally it was on a simple list of sayings.

Further evidence for the format of the Q document comes to us in the form of the Gospel of Thomas. Discovered in 1945 among the sands of the Egyptian desert at Nag Hammadi, Thomas is a list of over one hundred saying attributed to Jesus but lacking any context in which he said them. Therefore, we can say with certainty that such saying lists did exist in antiquity and can be confident that Q was of this type.

Q and Thomas also point to how the earliest stories of Jesus circulated before they came to be incorporated into the gospels. Jesus' sayings were first transferred orally between the first believers and were only later written down. Indeed, there is a precedent of this type of oral teaching in Judaism of this period. Sooner or later, the original followers of Jesus were dying out and someone thought it prudent to record these sayings in a list-like format. During the mid first century these saying documents were used to complete the first gospels.

The first gospels were written down on papyrus, a material that naturally disintegrates with handling, so every once in a while the words had to be copied onto new sheets. During this process some errors did occur. From surviving papyrus texts scholars can actually see that there were variations between texts, not least because the ancients were also bad spellers. The scribes might have also used this process as an opportunity to 'correct' certain theological points about Jesus from earlier versions and bring them up to date with the current belief system. This is best seen from the earliest surviving manuscripts of Mark, which ends after Jesus' death with the discovery of the empty tomb. In later versions this ending is drastically different. Not only is the empty tomb discovered but now Jesus actually re-appears to the disciples and tells them to go into the world and *"preach the good news to all creation,"*[14] a sentiment that most likely reflected the practices of later Christians, like Paul, who were already actively spreading the news of Jesus. Thus, we can say that after the gospels were first written they later underwent a process of editing.

Like a game of Chinese whispers the original sayings of Jesus were first transmitted orally, later recorded, edited and translated, and copied over and over again by generations of scribes. At each stage, small errors occurred, sometimes by accident, sometimes on purpose. What we have today is a culmination of this two thousand year process and we must therefore be cautious when using the gospels as a source of accurate information about Jesus.

Can We Know Anything About
Jesus' Character From The Gospels?

The traditional image that many Christians hold of Jesus is a man at peace with himself, an unblemished, young, wise and handsome man with long hair and a beard. None of this is in any way historical. The gospels contain no physical description of Jesus whatsoever and for all we know the historical Jesus could have been obese. Nor do we know anything solid about his actual character and personality. Having said this it is still fascinating to read through the gospels to catch a glimpse of the man. Perhaps the most interesting character of Jesus is in the gospel of Mark. Overall, Mark's version of Jesus depicts a bold figure, who darts around the countryside exorcising

---

[14] Mark 16:15

demons and healing the sick through their own faith. He is more a man of action, and less a man of words. What is appealing about Mark's Jesus is that he is a three dimensional character who is prone to emotional outbursts at his dull disciples. With his own family he is dismissive and rather abrupt. Mark's Jesus is on an urgent mission and has little time for those who don't understand him. He often comes across as demanding, abrasive and even somewhat rude. But as his last days on earth draw to a close Mark's Jesus is genuinely distressed, genuinely sorrowful.

It is interesting that throughout Mark's account, Jesus is very secretive about his identity as the true messiah. The only beings to recognize his true nature are the demons that have possessed the sick. The disciples sometimes struggle to understand his message but nevertheless recognize him as being the Christ. To those that recognize him, such as a man he has just healed, Jesus commands them to be silent. Why should he be so secretive?

Scholars have argued that perhaps in Jesus' own lifetime he wasn't recognized as being the messiah but only after his death and apparent resurrection did people start calling him by this title. Mark's secretive Jesus is an attempt to answer his detractors who may have asked why no one believed Jesus to be the messiah during his lifetime.

Anyway, compare Mark's Jesus to the character of the man in John. Whereas Mark's Jesus is understated, John's is positively showy about his identity. John's Jesus has no qualms about announcing who he truly is and no desire to hide his true identity. Wherever John was compiling his account, Jesus had already assumed a divine aspect. He is not simply the messiah, he has transcended his humanity and is an everlasting deity.

Within the account, the Jews even accuse Jesus of blasphemy *"because you, a mere man, claim to be god."*[15] Mark's primitive Jesus lacks any aspect of divinity, he is called teacher and messiah and identified with the prophets of the past but he never claims to be God.

Mark's human Jesus and John's divine being are more clearly contrasted by Jesus' last words on the cross. Mark has his character nailed on the cross in genuine pain, he cries out in a loud voice *"my god, my god, why have you forsaken me?"*[16] This is a cry of a prophet betrayed by the lord, a cry of heartfelt grief that his mission has failed. It is the cry of anguish of a man breathing his last. Compare this to John's gospel. On the cross, Jesus asks for a drink and *"when he had received the drink, Jesus said, 'it is finished.' With that, he bowed his head and gave up his spirit."*[17] This Jesus is wholly more controlled, cool even. He accepts his fate knowing that it is all part of the plan. From this example it is clear that the character of Jesus has been transformed according to the bias of his biographer. Mark clearly saw a human being at work, while John saw much more. This was a result of their own belief about Jesus, but can we know nothing of his historical character from the gospels?

Amid all of the theological wordings of the gospels sometimes it is possible to get a taste of the man as he might have been. One point that illustrates this is when Jesus is being compared to John the Baptist. John it will be remembered held an especially important place in first century Israel for his teachings and his ascetic lifestyle eating nothing but bread and honey. John was a holy man who had rejected the trappings of society to live a fulfilling lifestyle in a cave near to the river Jordon. The

---

[15] John 10:33
[16] Mark 15:34
[17] John 19:30

Baptist's disciples in the gospels question Jesus asking him, *"how is it that we and the Pharisees fast but your disciples do not fast?"*[18] Jesus it seems was not fond of abstaining from eating and drinking. *"Here is a glutton and a drunkard, a friend of tax collectors and sinners,"*[19] others say of Jesus. He drinks. He eats. Why would a god derive any pleasure from earthly delights such as these?

Since this story seems to serve no overriding theological purpose, and because it might be contrived to be an embarrassment to the later hierarchy of the church, this makes Jesus the glutton and drunkard a possible historical reality that has survived the editing process. As we shall learn in the next chapter, Jesus too doesn't seem to have enjoyed a close relationship with his family, and he cannot even perform any miracles in his hometown of Nazareth. All of these examples meet the criteria of embarrassment, one of the tools commonly used by scholars in the quest for the historical Jesus that helps determine true incidences in Jesus' life from contrived ones. It is fascinating to think that something of the true nature of Jesus might actually be preserved in these ancient, corrupted and biased texts.

If we haven't been so influenced by the images of Jesus as a slim, pure skinned westernized man, it might be easier to imagine the Jesus of the gospels as being rather larger-than-life type of person, at home among prostitutes and sinners and 'the lost sheep of Israel' with a jug of wine at his side, prone to a quick bit of wisdom but critical of those who didn't understand him. This of course is a flight of fancy but nevertheless these are the glimpses of an alternative Jesus that are given in the gospels.

---

[18] Matthew 9:14
[19] Matthew 11:19

In the end, the gospels are varied in their portrayal of Jesus' life and teachings but where they do overall agree is important – the fact that he did have a mission, that he did go about the countryside teaching, that he did meet a premature end on the cross. Yet each gospel portrays a man who is not idle, but who travels extensively around the Galilee and Judea (and perhaps even Samaria). The synoptic gospels have him healing the sick; the blind, the lame and the lepers. He expels evil demons out from people. Jesus is portrayed as being a man of fame and his message attracts those from all over Israel, they come to be healed and to hear him speak, and they gaze in wonderment at his ability to perform miracles. These aspects of Jesus' life are so well attested, along with his execution, that they are likely to have preserved a memory of Jesus' true life. That is not to say that Jesus really could do miracles because, as we shall see in a later chapter, there were other Jewish holy men who could elicit miracles and they lived contemporary with Jesus.

Why Does Jesus Ride Two Donkeys?

The gospels are a fascinating genre of ancient writing. They are unhistorical, fallible, and contain certain oddities that cannot easily be explained away. To illustrate this point, there is an interesting incident that is recorded in the gospel of Matthew. Jesus has been wandering the lands and spreading his message to his fellow Jews. He is hailed as the messiah who has come to restore Israel and its people and usher in the awaited Kingdom of Heaven. His words must be true as he has worked nothing less than miracles- he has healed the sick and cast out evil demons. But his life is drawing to a close. Jesus knows that as he approaches the ancient city of Jerusalem that this will be his last trip. Ahead awaits only misery, pain and a humiliating death nailed to a Roman cross like a common criminal. The scene couldn't be more dramatic as he approaches the culmination of his life's work. The people assemble along the road to Jerusalem to cheer their savior on his last journey. He passes them by, the lord, seated on two donkeys.

This is the scene as preserved and handed down to us in Matthew, and the reader would be forgiven, quite rightly, for asking what Jesus Christ was doing on two donkeys. Why not simply ride one?

Matthew writes that Jesus has just instructed his followers thus; *"Go to the village ahead of you, and at once you will find a donkey tied there, with her colt by her. Untie them and bring them to me... The disciples went and did as Jesus had instructed them. They brought the donkey and the colt, placed their cloaks on them, and Jesus sat on them."*[20] It seems quite odd that a man would sit on two donkeys when he might simply have sat on one. It is a little too comical, but alas this is what Matthew is saying. So what is happening here? Did Matthew really believe that Jesus sat on two donkeys? Why?

The key to understanding the two donkey mystery can be found in the Old Testament itself. After Matthew tells us that Jesus mounted the donkeys he says that: *"This took place to fulfill what was spoken through the prophet: 'Say to the Daughter of Zion, See, your king comes to you, gentle and riding on a donkey, on a colt, the foal of a donkey.'"* Matthew is referring to the Book of Zechariah in the Jewish scriptures which was later incorporated into the accepted Christian canon. Zechariah is a prophet from the post- exile period, a time when the Jews are returning to their homelands after a long exile under the Babylonians and the book contains a prophetic vision of a new Israel in which God will return to live among his chosen people and cleanse

---

[20] Matthew 21:1-8

them of their sins. Christians, ancient and present, regard the Book of Zechariah as an important text that actually predicts the arrival of Jesus. And Matthew was evidently using the text in order to foresee how the messiah would arrive in Jerusalem. So what relevance does this have to donkeys?

Many biblical historians with a critical eye have understood Matthew's two donkey passage as being a misunderstanding of an ancient Hebrew rhetorical device called Parallelism. Parallelism in Hebrew literature was a way of emphasizing an object by repeating other known facts about it. To give another way of looking at it I might use a parallelism to refer to myself as thus; I am a person, a son, a son of a man. In the original prophecy of Zechariah there is reference to only one donkey but with this device the donkey is also a colt, the son of a donkey.

Matthew appears to have trouble understanding the intricacies of ancient Hebrew literature, perhaps because he himself is writing in Greek and reading from a Greek translation of the Jewish scriptures and he mistakenly understands the passage in Zechariah as referring to two donkeys. Although the rest of the Matthew presents a very Jewish outlook, during these times Koine Greek was the lingua franca of the eastern Roman Empire. Indeed all of the gospels in the New Testament were originally written in this international language. Evidence also suggests that even the Jews who were spread throughout the Empire used Greek as their mother tongue, read the Torah in Greek, and may have had very little familiarity with either Aramaic or Hebrew.

This two donkey incident is not just a simple curiosity because when we look into matters a little more thoroughly it allows us to glimpse something of

Matthew's motivation and methodology behind writing his gospel. Clearly he believed that Jesus was the long awaited messiah. And since the messiah was predicted in the texts of the Jewish scriptures, logically, in Matthew's mind, the scriptures must therefore contain biographical information about the life of Jesus. This is not a deliberate attempt to mislead his readers because Matthew truly believes that Jesus' life is predicted in the ancient books of Jewish religion. So when he misreads the prophecy as having two donkeys he naturally assumes this is what actually happened to the historical Jesus on his final approach to Jerusalem.

Furthermore, Matthew's donkey confusion has weightier consequences for those who profess that the gospels are accurate eye witness accounts to the life of Jesus. Christian tradition about the authorship of the gospel attributes it to Matthew, a repentant tax collector (hated then just as they are now) who joins the Jesus movement and is taken onboard as one of the all important twelve disciples. In the Christian apologetic view, the gospel of Matthew is a reliable, first-hand account by one of Jesus' closest followers. However, Matthew's misreading of Zechariah actually shows us that he was not present at these events. It would be absurd to suggest that a man could ride on two donkeys, and indeed the other gospels only present Jesus riding on one such creature.

Instead, this incident shows us how the gospels were written. Matthew and the other gospel writers actively turn to the Old Testament for evidence of Jesus' life, taking bits of prophecies written centuries previous and applying them to the life of Jesus. Indeed there are literally hundreds of references to the Old Testament scattered throughout the four gospels; evidence

Christians say that Jesus did fulfill the prophecies. Evidence, say the skeptics, that he did not.

Although this is a seemingly trivial incident it does lead us to be very cautious when evaluating the gospels as historical sources. It shows us that elements of Jesus' life were borrowed from other sources within the Jewish tradition and the authors of the gospels had specific theological points they were trying to express. From this example we can surmise that the authors are unlikely to have been present at the events they describe. But, if the gospels are biased accounts written by men who never met Jesus does that mean we can learn nothing about the historical Jesus? Not necessarily. When properly analyzed through critical eyes the gospels can in fact lead us to a few solid conclusions about Jesus. And we must analyze the gospels because despite all of their evangelical and theological glosses they are practically the only sources of information about the life of the man.

Are The Gospels For or Against Jewish Law?

There are many things that can influence a writer's interpretation of events. His or her political, religious and socio-economic status for example often skewer the perspective of even modern journalists trained in objectivity. Bias is a factor of the gospels because obviously the evangelists hold certain understandings of Jesus and they want us to share their views. They want to glorify his name and show us his incredible deeds and his powerful teaching. In many places, they actually re-interpret events according to their own bias and nowhere is this more evident than in the evangelists' handling of the Jewish law.

The Jewish law, as provided by the prophet Moses, governed all aspects of life for a pious Jews in antiquity. As these laws were provided by God and because the Jews were very pious these laws in Jesus' era were almost unanimously followed although there were different interpretations.

Later on, when Christianity is being proclaimed in the Roman Empire, some Christians argue that the law should not be bound to the Gentiles. The most famous proponent of this argument was Paul of Tarsus, who wanted a relaxation of the laws, especially regarding the issue of circumcision, to allow more Gentiles to convert.

The gospels were written at a time when arguments over whether Gentile Christians needed to be followed the law were rife. Jesus himself has nothing to say on the matter because he never set foot outside of the Jewish lands, and plausibly he never conceived that his movement would be proclaimed abroad. And this often-heated debate influenced the gospels. In some places, the evangelists have even inserted their own words into Jesus' mouth in order to bolster their own ideas. Here we shall see how issues of the law and the Gentiles had an impact on the gospels. In particular, the gospels of Mark and Matthew with their contrasting opinions of the law will be examined.

Mark is written by a Gentile and his account is tailored to a Gentile audience. A review of the text reveals several clues that are indicative of this. Mark has to explain to his Gentile audience the meaning of certain Aramaic words and clarify certain aspects of Judaism such as what 'Corban' means;[21] Any Jew of the period would have been able to explain its significance as a sacrifice or offering to God. Mark also has to explain the geography of the region for those who have never been there and in places he uses Latin rather than Greek.

Mark even has to explain the meaning of ritual hand washing:

---

[21] Mark 7.11

*"The Pharisees and some of the teachers of the law
who had come from Jerusalem gathered around Jesus
and saw some of his disciples eating food with hands
that were 'unclean,' that is, unwashed. (The Pharisees
and all the Jews do not eat unless they give their
hands a ceremonial washing, holding to the tradition
of the elders. When they come from the Marketplace
they do not eat unless they wash. And they observe
many other traditions, such as the washing of cups,
pitchers and kettles.)"[22]*

This presupposes that not only does his Gentile audience not understand hand washing in the context of Jewish ritual purity, but also these early Christians were not practicing it. Mark's community were, therefore, largely ignorant of the practices of concurrent Judaism and were unlikely to have followed the law.

Matthew, on the other hand, is the most Jewish of all the gospels. Scholars have posited that the author was himself a Jewish-Christian, of the type that would later find itself in direct competition with the early Orthodox Church that was championed by the Gentile Christians.

In Matthew's gospel, Jesus is portrayed as a new Moses. Jesus came out from Egypt, according to Matthew, as did Moses. Jesus, Matthew tells us, was taken there to avoid the massacre of innocent children in Bethlehem because King Herod did not want a future king of Israel to challenge him. The similarities between Jesus' and Moses' birth stories are evident. Moses was the most important Jewish prophet in the past and in Matthew's view Jesus was the most important now.

Matthew was certainly an expert on the scriptures, and there are in fact some sixty-five references to the Old Testament in his gospel, more than any of his

---

[22] Mark 7:1-4

colleagues. Since we can imagine that Matthew was a Jew it is not surprising that his version of Jesus is made to say the following:

"Do not think that I have come to abolish the Law or the Prophets; I have not come to abolish them but to fulfill them. I tell you the truth, until heaven and earth disappear, not the smallest letter, not the least stroke of a pen, will by any means disappear from the Law until everything is accomplished. Anyone who breaks one of the least of these commandments and teaches others to do the same will be called least in the kingdom of heaven, but whoever practices and teaches these commands will be called great in the kingdom of heaven. For I tell you that unless your righteousness surpasses that of the Pharisees and the teachers of the law, you will certainly not enter the kingdom of heaven."[23]

In Matthew's opinion, Jesus had not come to abolish the law. Not the smallest commandment was to be removed from it. Therefore, we can easily imagine in Matthew's community there were Jews who believed in Jesus but were still bound by the law. We can argue that they were observing the Kosher food laws and circumcising their sons.

Contrast Matthew's statement that the law is still binding with what Mark has to say on the matter:

"Again Jesus called the crowd to him and said, 'Listen to me, everyone, and understand this. Nothing outside a man can make him 'unclean' by going into him. Rather, it is what comes out of a man that makes him 'unclean.' For it doesn't go into his heart but into his

---

[23] Matthew 5:17-20

stomach, and then out of his body (in saying this, Jesus declared all foods clean.)"[24]

It is quite obvious that Mark has inserted his own ideas into his gospel by making Jesus declare that all foods were now clean. This simple statement diminishes the Kosher food laws that were commanded by Moses, and is in complete contradiction to Matthew's statement that the Jewish law was still binding on all. Mark's statement is not an accurate representation of the historical Jesus but is merely the opinion of the author. In his view, the law was no longer binding and he consequently slants this story of Jesus to reflect his beliefs. If the historical Jesus in his native context had acted in the manner described by Mark the scandal would have been immense. These were the laws of God and it is impossible to imagine Jesus gaining a following of Jews if he had actually said these things.

Historically speaking, Jesus as a first century Jew is more likely to have followed and interpreted the law than to have dismissed it, as Mark insists that he did. It is unlikely that Jesus would have dared to prohibit circumcision among his followers. As we shall see in the next chapter, Jesus' very own brother still wanted the Kosher laws to be binding upon the Gentile converts, which shows that there was a continuation of the Mosaic Law into the Christian era among certain Jewish Christians.

Conclusions

To summarize this chapter it is enough to say that the gospels do not present us with the kind of solid history, which we might expect from a modern biography concerning a famous or important person. Perhaps it is going too far to even consider them biographies in the

---

[24] Mark 7:14-19

strictest sense, because the gospels are so loaded with theological interpretations that have blurred any objectivity that once might have existed. The gospels are works written by men with a clear aim of promoting their own religious views of Jesus.

Matthew still sat comfortably within the first Jewish-Christian movements which we know continued for centuries more, while his counterpart Mark was a Gentile writing to other non-Jews possibly from Rome itself. If we are to be objective observers of them, like a police detective, then we can easily detect their background has biased their accounts. Thus Matthew appears to be rather more pro-law than Mark.

Meanwhile, a review of the gospels shows how they were written. Jesus' sayings and teachings were not immediately recorded, but circulate orally for a period of time until eventually they are written down and incorporated into a biography of sorts which we call a gospel. As they have gone through centuries of translation and transmission we have to be careful because some aspects are not original to Jesus. Words have been placed into his mouth by later editors who have something to say.

Christians have often ignored the background of the gospels and have taken their content as divinely inspired truth. It is a mistake simply to take the gospels at face value because there are so many influences that have shaped them so that in the end we simply do not know whether Jesus uttered any of the words attributed to him. While this is not a problem for a person of faith, the critical historian must attempt to reconstruct a world in which Jesus lived and decide whether he could have said those words in that setting.

Some aspects of Jesus life story, as represented in the gospels, have also suffered from exaggeration, or a reinterpretation and we saw how Matthew used ancient prophecy to shape his account of Jesus' entry into Jerusalem. Jesus' story has been given additional color over the years and nowhere is this more evident than in the story of his birth, which we shall now explore.

CHAPTER THREE

When God is a Child

Supposedly, it was St. Francis of Assisi who held the first ever nativity play in 1223. For the performance he used actors as well as live animals and the show was a hit. It was given the official stamp of approval by the Pope and within a century every church in Italy was hosting similar plays. It is a testament to the popularity of this annual ritual that it has survived through the Middle Ages and continues to be a feature of Christmas celebration all the way down to our own, increasingly secular time. Certainly the common elements of the nativity will be familiar to even the most ardent skeptic or atheist. We all know that Jesus was supposedly born on the 25th of December and that his parents were making a journey to Bethlehem but they could find nowhere to stay, even the inn was full and so the holy mother gave birth to her son in a humble manger. Then there was the star that guided three wise men (or were they kings?) from the east all the way to the stable.

Alas, the skeptics with their drive for the truth have to conclude that all of this is a myth. Indeed nowhere in the gospels does it say that the star hovered over the barn in which Jesus was born, only that the magi saw a sign in the sky. They also don't tell us that there were three wise men- there could have been thirty for all we can tell from the gospels. Moreover, there are no adoring donkeys. Images of the ox and ass at the stable in fact derive from an apocryphal work, the gospel of pseudo Matthew, written much later in the eighth or ninth century. The author of this gospel had also pinched elements from the Old Testament to give his account some color. In this case, the ox and ass were taken from the book of Isaiah.

These days, even liberal Christians will agree with the notion that much of Jesus' birth is legendary, but we have cherished the myths of Jesus' birth for so long that they are hard to put down and forget. We like the story and the story has remained. Indeed, if generations of Christians stuck strictly to scripture then our modern school plays would be considerably more boring.

Another important aspect of the nativity scene that is tough to be rid of is Mary and her virginity. Jesus' mother was so pure that she had never been with a man and the Catholic Church teaches that she remained a virgin for the rest of her life. Since the earliest church first began codifying and standardizing their beliefs the virgin birth has been an essential component. From the Apostle's Creed in the fourth century up until the Small Catechism of Martin Luther of 1529, Christians have officially maintained that Jesus was born of a virgin called Mary. Even today, all one has to do is read some pro-Christian websites to understand the veracity of the defense of the virgin birth. Why is it so important? Why can't Christians revere Jesus without a virgin mother?

In this chapter we shall examine the beliefs of Christians regarding Jesus and his birth, but also examine something of his early life, his birthplace and his family. Just like the nativity scene, much of what we imagine Jesus' early life to be is a mere myth. Like so much of his story, someone thousands of years ago wanted us to believe that Jesus was very special indeed. When the gospels were being compiled towards the end of the first century the authors believe that the Jewish messiah had descended upon the world in the form of Jesus - a man that none of the authors had ever met. If we remember that these gospels are not objective reports, but biased theological compositions, we must then ask how much of the information relating to Jesus' birth and life is historical, and how much, like the nativity play, is fanciful?

Was Jesus Descended From David?

Within the Judaism of the Roman era there was a common belief that the messiah would be a man descended from the royal bloodline of David, based on the promise God had made to the fabled king. The community who left behind the Dead Sea Scrolls were for example expecting a Davidic messiah. A fragment known as 4Q285, part of a series dealing with a war of the messiah, does indeed corroborate this. Even today there are Jews awaiting a Davidic messiah.

The gospels were written by authors who believe that Jesus was this long awaited figure and they are therefore quite keen to show us that Jesus possessed the right credentials for the job- in other words they wanted to demonstrate that Jesus was a direct descendent of David. To satisfy this prerequisite, two of the gospels include a genealogy of Jesus that traces his ancestry all the way back to David himself.

On the first page of the gospel of Matthew we are presented with a genealogy that traces Jesus' roots through David and all the way back to Abraham. Luke similarly thinks it necessary to establish Jesus' credentials and also includes a genealogy. Unfortunately for proponents of biblical inerrancy, the two genealogies are completely different from each other.

The Genealogy of Jesus According To Matthew

1	Abraham	15	Solomon	29	Shealtiel
2	Isaac	16	Rehoboam	30	Zerubbabel
3	Jacob	17	Abijam	31	Abiud
4	Judah	18	Asa	32	Eliakim
5	Pharez	19	Jehoshaphat	33	Azor
6	Hezron	20	Jehoram	34	Zadok
7	Ram	21	Uzziah	35	Achim
8	Amminadab	22	Jotham	36	Eliud
9	Nahshon	23	Ahaz	37	Eleazar
10	Salmon	24	Hezekiah	38	Matthan
11	Boaz	25	Manasseh	39	Jacob
12	Obed	26	Amon	40	Joseph
13	Jesse	27	Josiah	41	Jesus
14	David	28	Jeconiah		

The Genealogy of Jesus According To Luke

1	God	29	Amminadab	57	Zerubbabel
2	Adam	30	Nasshon	58	Rheas
3	Seth	31	Salmon	59	Joanan
4	Enosh	32	Boaz	60	Joda
5	Cainain	33	Obed	61	Josech
6	Mahalalel	34	Jesse	62	Semein
7	Jared	35	David	63	Mattathias
8	Enoch	36	Nathan	64	Maath
9	Methuselah	37	Mattatha	65	Naggai
10	Lamech	38	Menna	66	Esli
11	Noah	39	Melea	67	Nahum
12	Shem	40	Eliakim	68	Amos
13	Arphaxad	41	Jonam	69	Mattathias
14	Cainan	42	Joseph	70	Joseph
15	Shelah	43	Judah	71	Jannai
16	Eber	44	Simeon	72	Melki
17	Peleg	45	Levi	73	Levi
18	Reu	46	Matthat	74	Matthat
19	Serug	47	Jorim	75	Heli
20	Nahor	48	Eliezer	76	Joseph
21	Terah	49	Joshua	77	Jesus
22	Abraham	50	Er		
23	Isaac	51	Elmadam		
24	Jacob	52	Cosam		
25	Judah	53	Addi		
26	Pharez	54	Melki		
27	Hezron	55	Neri		
28	Ram	56	Shealtiel		

The first notable difference between these two versions is that Matthew traces Jesus' roots back to Abraham while Luke follows it all the way back to the very first human being, Adam, and ultimately to God. Why each version has a different emphasis provides us with a fascinating insight into their cultural bias. We have already demonstrated that Matthew's gospel is much more Jewish in nature, and that Jesus has come to fulfill the law and not destroy it; so it is interesting that he should trace Jesus' lineage back to Abraham –the founding father of the Israelite nation. Luke, on the other hand, was writing for a Gentile audience and so chooses to follow Jesus' line all the way back to the very first human, Adam, who was understood to be the common ancestor to all of humanity, and not just to the Jews. So, whereas Luke is saying that Jesus' message applies to both Jew and Gentile, Matthew has him primarily working towards a Jewish mission.

Matthew's genealogy has a great emphasis on the number fourteen. After he has presented his list of names he tells us:

> *"Thus there were fourteen generations in all from Abraham to David, fourteen from David to the exile to Babylon, and fourteen from the exile to the Christ."*[25]

Indeed all of the names presented at the magical fourteen mark are significant in the history of Israel; David redeeming Israel represents the first fourteen. Jeconiah, a Judean king, was deposed by the Babylonians and his people sent into exile are at the end of the next set of fourteen. And the last name is of course Jesus whom Matthew believes will usher in the Kingdom of Heaven, a time when heavenly justice will prevail on earth. But Matthew makes a mistake. If you

---

[25] Matthew 1:17

look closely From Jeconiah to Jesus, there are in fact only thirteen generations. Matthew has just told us that there are fourteen. This error is strange since Matthew has taken particular care when copying the list of names from the Book of Chronicles in the Old Testament to make sure that his own numerological emphasis is followed. He even cuts out several names from that genealogy in order for his own list to match with the all important number fourteen. You would expect him to check his numbers more closely.

Why the particular interest in the number fourteen anyway? Scholars have speculated that the number is significant because it represents David's number. In ancient alphabets letters could also represent numerals, thus A might mean one, and B would be two. An example of this is in the book of Revelations where the number 666 is given as the number of the beast (this number represents a name although there is much speculation as to who is being referred to, possibly the Roman Emperor Nero). Anyway, if you added up all of the consonants of David's name in the Hebrew alphabet (remembering that they didn't count vowels) you would arrive at the number fourteen. Matthew's use of numerology is another way of suggesting that Jesus does have a significant connection with David.

Luke's genealogy is different in many respects to that of Matthew's. Firstly, his list appears in a different part of the narrative; in Luke, the genealogy is presented after Jesus' baptism by John, while Matthew's is given just before Jesus' birth. Besides this, there are names given in Luke that do not appear in his counterpart's work. At least one of these is significant in trying to understand Luke's motivation in presenting this list. Luke includes the name Nathan which is absent from Matthew. Nathan is not well known in the greater history of the bible but he is mentioned in the Old Testament and is described as a 'son of god'. This title and its true meaning in this era will be analyzed in the next chapter but suffice to say Luke evidently was trying to show off Jesus' credentials as another son of god, or indeed the ultimate son of god since he is the last on the list.

Furthermore, Luke's list contains fewer names in his genealogy - From Abraham to Jesus there are just forty one names while in Matthew this same lineage contains fifty five. You would expect believers of the inerrancy of the bible to meet a hurdle at this point where even liberal Christians surmise that at least one of the evangelists has made a mistake.

The genealogies are counted from male generations, thus in Matthew; *"matthan [was] the father of Jacob, and Jacob the father of Joseph, the husband of Mary, of whom was born Jesus."* But Matthew then runs into another problem; he has just presented his genealogy and then he continues to describe how Mary the mother of Jesus had given birth without the usual method of conception. Mary is a virgin. This leads us to an interesting dilemma for the evangelists - how on earth can Jesus claim to be of the royal bloodline of David if he has no earthly father?

Neither author tries to answer this problem though they both present the genealogy of Jesus and the virgin birth. Recognizing this error later Christian apologists have tried to come up with suitable answers. Tertullian in the second century said that Jesus is descended from David through the bloodline of Mary. This doesn't help much because the genealogies are not matriarchal. They specifically count only the male of each generation. Others have speculated that Jesus' stepfather was a descendent of David and when he married Mary that bloodline somehow passed onto Jesus. All of these explanations are unconvincing to an objective historian but this question continues to raise great debate among the believers.

The genealogies are in effect a type of propaganda. They contain no solid evidence for Jesus' bloodline and we therefore have to treat them with a heavy dose of skepticism. What they instead show, is how the evangelists wanted us to believe Jesus was a descendent of David and therefore was the messiah. And they achieved this through adding the genealogies. We can trust the genealogies as historical sources only as far as we can trust Matthew's statement that Jesus rode two donkeys in to Jerusalem, put in another way – they tell us nothing about the historical Jesus' bloodline.

Was Mary Really A Virgin?

Thanks to the belief that Mary was a virgin, Jesus' mother has experienced her own elevation beyond that of a normal saint. If anything, she is practically a deity herself. Mary's own divine veneration is seen in 1453 for example when the Turks had assembled a massive force and were laying siege to the last strand of the Byzantium Empire. In defense of Constantinople, Emperor Constantine XI relied on massive walls supported by canon and crossbows but the Muslim attack was relentless. There was however another line of defense. Each day the religious leaders took from the churches images of the Virgin Mary and paraded them along the walls. Surely Mary, the mother of God and the patron saint of Constantinople would deflect the heathen bombardment and save her loyal Christian subjects. Alas, it was not to be. The Turks succeeded and Constantinople became a Muslim city as it is to this day.

By this stage of history, Mary had developed her own form of divinity as the desperate pleas from the faithful defenders would attest. Arguably it was the virgin birth and the belief in her perpetual virginity that propelled Mary to god-like status. It was the Gentile church that first began to revere Mary. The former pagans having rejected their old pantheon of gods found the lack of a mother goddess figure disquieting and Mary seemed like the best replacement. One merely need to regard a statue of the Egyptian goddess Isis seated with a child in her hand and compare it to Christian depictions of the virgin Mary with the infant Jesus to see the striking similarities. And as Christianity spread and lay down roots around the Mediterranean, the new mother goddess increasingly took over old cultic sites, effectively replacing pagan images with Christian ones. Her veneration continues today as a saint in the Catholic Church - believers offer prayers to her statues and the blessed virgin continues to make return trips to Earth, appearing to the faithful in everything from spectacular mass visions like that at Fatima in 1917 to humble images in potato chips.

Alas, we know all too little about the historical Mary other than a few mentions here and there in the gospels. A woman by the name of Mary might have existed since the historical Jesus would certainly have needed a mother, and Mary was a fairly common name in those times. Surely, she had to have been a normal girl of the age, with a husband and a child - how then did she come to attain a status second to none in the mother goddess department?

It is possible that the reason for her veneration can be attributed to nothing less than a shaky Greek translation of the Old Testament in a crucial passage that anticipates the coming messiah. Before we get to this point it must be remembered that the gospels were originally written in Greek. We know from textual analysis of the gospels that the authors were using a

Greek version of the Old Testament known to scholars as the Septuagint.

Originally completed before 132 BCE, the Septuagint was held in high esteem by both Jews and Gentiles alike. Furthermore, this version was divinely inspired; according to legend seventy-two translators worked in separate rooms for seventy two days and after they found that they had all written the exact same work! A modern appraisal of the Septuagint reveals quite a few differences between it and the original Hebrew version contained in the Masoretic text. These minor discrepancies in translation would prove no hurdling block to the gospel writers, however, because they had in their hands the divine, definitive Greek version while they considered the Hebrew as uninspired and consequently rejected it.

One of these minor differences is all important to the case of Mary's virgin birth and has courted controversy over its exact meaning by mainstream Christians. 'Alamah' is a Hebrew noun meaning a young girl who is of the age to marry. This is the word that is used in the Masoretic version of Isaiah 7.14, a critical passage held by Christians as actually predicting the birth of Jesus. In the Septuagint version, the Hebrew 'alamah' is translated into Greek 'parthenos', a word that means virgin in the sense that we would usually understand it today. Put simply, the original Hebrew prophecy mentions a girl, but in the Greek Septuagint version the girl in question is specifically a virgin. This has caused a great deal of biblical skeptics to point out that Matthew's version of events derive from this mistranslation. In effect, Matthew was not reporting events that had happened, but was reconstructing what he thought had happened based on the Greek version of his Old Testament.

To counter this, Christians have claimed that 'alamah' also means 'a virgin', but this assertion is problematic because the proper Hebrew word for virgin is 'bethulah.' The author of Isaiah does in fact use 'bethulah' five times elsewhere in the book in connection with virgins. Surely he would have used it to signify that the woman in the prophecy was indeed a virgin if that was what his original message intended.

Meanwhile, a proper reading of Isaiah reveals that he is focused on events that are occurring in his own time, eighth century BCE Judea, and is concerned that the Jewish people are ignoring monotheism and practicing idolatry. Quite ironic then that later generations of Christians would use his passage as a basis for their own veneration of Mary which Isaiah would have considered both blasphemous and idolatrous.

The Isaiah passage sparks great debate and controversy among Christians in the modern era. For example, the Revised Standard Version (RSV) of the bible caused massive consternation within certain churches in the deep American South simply because it had attempted to accurately translate the Old Testament into English and had chosen to translate 'alamah' into its proper English form - a young girl. One pastor was so enraged by this that he took up a blowtorch and burnt the RSV bible from his pulpit and then sent the ashes to Luther Weigle, who had worked as a translator on the project.

The virgin birth had grown to be such an important aspect in the faith of Christianity that it would not easily be done away with. But why was it so important? Why couldn't Jesus be both born of a human mother and be the messiah at the same time? Why did he need a special birth?

The answer perhaps lies within the Greco-Roman appetite for explaining extraordinary men through miraculous births. The legendary figures of Asclepius,

Hercules and Dionysus all had human mothers and divine fathers. Historical figures, among them mighty rulers and wise philosophers, seemed to have been singled out for miracle conceptions. An example is the famous philosopher Plato. There are several ancient accounts of his legendary birth which commonly have Apollo appearing in a vision to Plato's mother who then becomes pregnant, despite the fact that she has yet to lay with her husband. The god's were certainly busy in those times, but having a divine birth did help the ancients to explain and understand why some men were greater than others. The miraculous birth of Jesus would have helped the Gentiles throughout the Empire to understand that Jesus was a great man; like Plato and Pythagoras, like Alexander the Great and Julius Caesar, Jesus too had experienced a miraculous birth. The power and wisdom of these men far outpaced that of their contemporaries and was explained away by assigning them an extraordinary birth. Their deeds were so great that they were understood to have shared in some aspect of the divine.

Interestingly, the early Christians might have used the example of a miraculous birth to help convert their pagan neighbors who were well acquainted with the legendary births of their heroes. The church father Origen (185–254 CE) wrote numerous theological treaties concerning Jesus and his divinity. In his refutation of the Celsus heresy, he writes *"it is not absurd to employ Greek stories to talk with Greeks, to show we Christians are not the only people who use a miraculous story like this one [Jesus' own birth]."*[26] Since we do know that the gospels were written for a Gentile audience it is easy to suggest that reasoning like Celsus' would have helped to propagate the myth of Mary's virginity into the modern era.

---

[26] Against Celsus, 1.37

Even Matthew, whose gospel is considerably more Jewish in nature, would have been familiar with the idea of miracle births because he was most likely writing from within the Empire. Could he have inserted this story to help convert his pagan countrymen? This is speculation of course, although the story of Jesus' birth would have also struck a chord with the Jews of the age. In the scriptures we read of Isaac, the poor boy who narrowly escaped being sacrificed to God by his hundred year old father. Isaac was born from a barren mother just like other prophets such as Jacob and Samuel. In each of these cases, the will of God allowed their mothers to conceive though they were physically incapable of becoming pregnant and in each case their offspring would continue to lead outstanding lives.

Outside of Luke and Matthew, the historicity of the virgin birth lacks multiple attestations. Not only does the earliest gospel, Mark, contain no mention of it, no virgin birth appears in any of Paul's letters. Paul's writings are the earliest Christian works in the New Testament and the absence of the miraculous birth story suggests that it was simply not a feature of his beliefs. In his letter to the Galatians he says merely; *"God sent forth his son born of a woman, born under the law."*[27] If anything, Paul, as our earliest witness, is stressing the human nature of Jesus and his mother in this passage.

With these things in mind it seems highly unlikely that the historical Mary had anything approaching a miraculous birth. The story is a myth, a strong myth that survives among congregations of Christians two thousand years later, but a myth all the same.

---

[27] Galatians 4:4

Was Jesus Born in Bethlehem or Nazareth?

The gospel stories (as well as school nativity plays) represent Jesus being born in Bethlehem. Why then is he popularly known as Jesus of Nazareth? Wouldn't Jesus of Bethlehem be a more appropriate title for him? The problem is further expanded when reading through the gospels we hear of numerous references to Jesus coming from Nazareth.

In the gospel of John, Jesus has just invited Philip to join him in his work. Philip is excited about the prospect and then tells his friend Nathanael *"We have found the one Moses wrote about in the Law, and about whom the prophets also wrote – Jesus of Nazareth, the son of Joseph."* Nathanael is more than a little confused about this and says *"Nazareth! Can anything good come from there?"*[28]

When we remember that the Galilee was largely an agricultural area and the people were often regarded as being rough then Nathanael's objections make more sense. Another example from John has a crowd of people ask themselves, *"How can the Christ come from the Galilee? Does not scripture say that the Christ will come from David's family and from Bethlehem?"*[29] Certainly the people in John's gospel believe Jesus to be from the Galilee and they are confused as to how he could both be a Galilean and be the messiah at the same time. This incident possibly preserves an early strain of doubt among Jews regarding Jesus' messianic claim. If Jesus actually had been born in Bethlehem then this argument would not have arisen.

The key to understanding why the gospel authors wanted their central character born in Bethlehem is once again linked in with their perception of Jesus as the

---

[28] John 1:45-46
[29] John 7:41

messiah. Bethlehem was the town in Judea in which David was crowned king and the Jews expected the messiah to emerge from that kingly city. The relevant Old Testament passage concerning the birth of the messiah in Bethlehem is in Micah. Elsewhere, the text is predicting a guerrilla leader who would rise out of Bethlehem to wage war and defeat the Assyrians. This warrior would offer no mercy against the foreign infidels in the protection of Judea. Seeing the prophecy of Micah in this its original context makes it hard to see how Jesus could have fulfilled it- he was neither a guerrilla warlord nor did he defeat the Assyrians. This is yet another example of how the evangelist scoured through the Old Testament, picking and choosing prophecies and adapting them to their gospels. Nevertheless, it is the town of Bethlehem that is important here and the gospel writers are keen to have their character born in the correct place to further bolster his messianic claim.

Yet in their haste to have Jesus of Nazareth born in Bethlehem the gospel writers have a lot of explaining to do. Luke weaves a semi-historical story to get Jesus born in the right place. He tells us that:

> *"In those days Caesar Augustus issued a decree that a census should be taken of the entire Roman world. (This was the first census that took place while Quirinius was governor of Syria.)And everyone went to his own town to register. So Joseph also went up from the town of Nazareth in Galilee to Judea, to Bethlehem the town of David, because he belonged to the house and line of David. He went there to register with Mary, who was pledged to be married to him and was expecting a child."* [30]

---

[30] Luke 2:1-6

Thus, Luke is saying that because Joseph was a descendent of David he had to travel all the way to Bethlehem to register. The journey from Nazareth in the Galilee to Bethlehem in Judea was not an easy one. If they were travelling as the crow flied the journey would have been at least 80 miles long, but on the rocky roads and mountainous trails it would have been considerably longer. They would have had to have passed through the hostile lands of the Samaritans while also being weary of the numerous bandits that Josephus tells us were a common occurrence in these times. For a heavily pregnant woman the journey would have been uncomfortable and extremely dangerous.

Historically speaking, there was a census a couple of years after Jesus' birth - the Census of Quirnius dated to 6 or 7 CE. When the Romans took control of Judea and Samaria they wanted to know how much the people possessed so they could be appropriately taxed. The historical census might have worked in a similar way as to when the Norman invaders of Saxon England compiled the Doomsday Book, which recorded how many households were within a settlement and how many animals were in each village. To achieve this it would have been practical to send out agents around the land to visit each settlement and compile a report. The gospels paint a different methodology for the Census of Quirnius, however. Luke says the Emperor wanted a census of the whole Roman world and that every person was expected to leave their land and return to their ancestral homeland to register themselves. Luke's version is both impractical and implausible - The Romans were interested in a quick survey of the newly acquired territory for tax purposes but the upheaval resulting from several million people travelling miles away to register would have interrupted their daily work and the imperial coffers would surely suffer. Poor Joseph is made to embark on a hazardous journey from his village simply because forty-two generations ago his distant ancestor, David, had lived in Bethlehem! This naturally strikes the gospel skeptic as a highly unlikely occurrence and entirely impractical to the Roman governance of its empire. A final problem with the historicity of this story arises because at the time of the census the Galilee, where Nazareth is located and where Jesus' parents were living, was not yet under direct Roman control. It was still being administered by one of King Herod's sons and would have fallen beyond the scope of Quirnius' census.

As if Luke's version wasn't difficult enough, Matthew's Jesus takes a different and even longer route to be born. According to Matthew, the family had already made it to Bethlehem but now the gospel writer has to explain what the messiah was doing in Nazareth later in his life. The story goes that the holy family had to get out of Bethlehem because of the murderous intentions of Herod who wanted to massacre all the innocent children in the town due to a prophecy that one of them would become king of the Jews. To escape the slaughter, Joseph takes his wife and child all the way to Egypt. When Herod dies they are then free to return but thanks to Herod's successor who is ruling in Judea they decide to settle down in the Galilee and stay out of trouble for as long as possible. Matthew uses this trip as an opportunity to relate Jesus to the prophet Moses, both should have been killed at birth, both came out from Egypt and both would redeem the Jewish people.

Aside from these flimsy birth narratives most of the evidence suggests that Jesus spent most of his time in and around the Galilee. There are several examples in the gospels where Jesus is identified as a Galilean or a Nazarene and historically speaking there is no reason to suspect that Jesus was born anywhere else. Years after his birth, his evangelical biographers perpetrated the myth that he was born in Bethlehem in order to highlight his role as the messiah.

What is it Like Being a Child God?

Today any biography is incomplete without some knowledge of the childhood of its subject. Thus a biography of Adolf Hitler when demonstrating that the young Adolf was beaten by his father gives us an understanding to his later aggressive and paranoid psychology. Jesus' childhood is largely not dealt with at all in the gospels, not because they are incomplete, but simply because the ancients chose only to highlight the important aspects of a man's life that were directly connected with their achievements. The four canonical gospels do not give us much information about the child Jesus because in their view his actions in adult life were far more important to understanding the man.

Being born into a Jewish family, however, would have meant that Jesus would have been circumcised, and in Luke we see precisely this when he tells us that on the eight day Jesus was circumcised in keeping with the law. Additionally, the infant Jesus would have been presented to the temple, as Luke explains: *"When the time of their purification according to the Law of Moses had been completed, Joseph and Mary took him to Jerusalem to present him to the Lord (as it is written in the Law of the Lord, "Every firstborn male is to be consecrated to the Lord"), and to offer a sacrifice in keeping with what is said..."*[31] Despite later Christian reflection that Jesus had subverted the Mosaic Law, the virgin Mary evidently saw the need to stick with tradition, perhaps she wasn't as Christian as they have assumed.

---

[31] Luke 2:22-24

The only incident of Jesus' childhood recorded by the gospels is narrated by Luke; Mary and Joseph suddenly realize that they have lost their son and search all over for him, only to find him within the Temple and conversing quite well with the rabbis there. None of the other gospels contain this story, so its historicity is unlikely but instead is intended to demonstrate Jesus' extraordinary gifts even at that young age.

There is a tradition that Joseph was a carpenter and that Jesus had learned something of this profession during his early years. His working background had helped people imagine his humble beginnings, but the images of a young Jesus learning to cut wood in his father's workshop are not very strongly attested in the gospels. The terms 'Jesus' and 'carpenter' are only placed together in one sentence from all of the gospels. Meanwhile, the translation of the word 'carpenter' rests on the Greek 'ho tekton' which is used to designate the Aramaic 'aram naggar.' This can mean a carpenter but could also be used to designate a craftsman, a scholar or some kind of learned man. Perhaps Jesus wasn't born into a working family at all. Perhaps, they were rather more educated. It is safer to say that we do not know what the historical father of Jesus would have done to provide for his family and we also know nothing of Jesus' upbringing.

There are several apocryphal gospels that attempt to fill in the blanks about Jesus' early life. Centuries after Jesus' death, when Christianity has taken root already, people begin to wonder as to what it would be like for a child divinity growing up. Most of these works were rejected as being heretical and they are much too late to be considered accurate history but they are nevertheless important in demonstrating that there were many alternative beliefs and sects within early Christianity. Besides, they make an interesting read.

The Infancy Gospel of Thomas is dated approximately to the end of the second or early third century and is one such apocryphal work that explores what it was like for the young Jesus. What was it like for the Son of God growing up? What did he do with his powers? This intriguing gospel gives us the answer: Jesus was a somewhat troublesome child who did not get on well with the other children. One boy even punched the young lord (alternative texts have a child throwing a stone or bumping into Jesus) who retaliates by cursing him. The boy withered away and died. The dead boy's parents were of course distraught and they came to Mary and Joseph to complain. To get out of a tricky situation, the young Jesus turned them blind. A less sinister incident in the gospel has Jesus molding a clay model of a bird with his hands. When he blows into it, miraculously it comes to life and flies away.

Although the church rejected these alternative gospels they still held a cherished place in the community that read and studied them, and it is fascinating to think that some of these stories are still in circulation and revered to this day, as this example from the Quran demonstrates:

> "O Jesus, son of Mary, remember My blessings upon
> you and your mother. I supported you with the Holy
> Spirit, to enable you to speak to the people from the
> crib, as well as an adult. I taught you the scripture,
> wisdom, the Torah, and the Gospel. Recall that you
> created from clay the shape of a bird by My leave, then
> blew into it, and it became a live bird by My leave."[32]

Jesus' clay birds must have been a popular story at the time for it to be incorporated by the Prophet Mohammed into the Muslim holy book.

---

[32] Quran 5:110

Why Does Jesus' Family Think He is Mad?

Another hurdle in for those who believe in the perpetual virginity of Mary is that fact that Jesus had a family consisting of several brothers and sisters. Evangelicals who hold that Mary was always a virgin have rejected Jesus' siblings by explaining them away as children from Joseph's earlier marriage but it is easier for a historian simply to assume that the historical Jesus would have had siblings. That he did have brothers is widely attested in the sources and some even went on to hold positions of prominence in the early church, especially among the earliest Jewish-Christian movement based in Jerusalem.

From the gospels we learn the names of his brothers; James, Judas and Simon but he also has several sisters who are not mentioned by name. Mark says that Jesus is their brother, which implies they were blood relatives; however those trying to distance themselves from this assumption have argued that the term 'brother' is not what we might understand today, that a brother could also mean a cousin. Either way, Jesus has a family, a father and mother and several siblings and this is certainly historically plausible and even very likely considering that many pre-industrial societies had large families.

When we reflect on traditional Christian teachings about the importance of families then one might be surprised when reading the gospels to see how Jesus gets on with his own relations. Throughout the accounts, his relatives are portrayed negatively - they are disbelievers, they think Jesus is mad and Jesus does not accept them. Indeed he even seems to prefer his own disciples over his family. Here is an example from Mark: *"When his family heard about this, they went to take charge of him, for they said, 'He is out of his mind.'"*[33] It seems that Jesus' family was

---

[33] Mark 3:21

concerned about their inerrant son who had lost his mind and sought to keep him in check. A little later in the text this incident occurs:

> *"A crowd was sitting around him, and they told him,*
> *'Your mother and brothers are outside looking for you.'*
> *'Who are my mother and my brothers?' he asked. Then*
> *he looked at those seated in a circle around him and*
> *said, 'Here are my mother and my brothers! Whoever*
> *does God's will is my brother and sister and mother.'"*[34]

'Who are my mother and brothers?' is the rude reply to the crowd. Outside of the synoptic tradition John also contains echoes of a disunions family life:

> *"After this, Jesus went around in Galilee, purposely*
> *staying away from Judea because the Jews there were*
> *waiting to take his life. But when the Jewish Feast of*
> *Tabernacles was near, Jesus' brothers said to him, 'You*
> *ought to leave here and go to Judea, so that your*
> *disciples may see the miracles you do. No one who wants*
> *to become a public figure acts in secret. Since you are*
> *doing these things, show yourself to the world.' For even*
> *his own brothers did not believe in him."*[35]

His failure to impress with his miracles is not confined only to close family members. Indeed, he finds that he has no miraculous powers whatsoever in his hometown of Nazareth and the villagers are doubtful of him. They ask: *"'Isn't this the carpenter? Isn't this Mary's son and the brother of James, Joseph, Judas and Simon? Aren't his sisters here with us?' And they took offense at him. Jesus said to them, 'Only in his hometown, among his relatives and in his own house is a prophet without honor.' He could not do any miracles there, except lay his hands on a few sick people and heal them. And he was amazed at their lack of faith."*[36] Jesus

---

[34] Mark 3:32-35
[35] John 7:1-5
[36] Mark 6:3-5

is consistently shown to have a less than close relationship with his family and those in his hometown. Does this imply a historical truth?

There is an argument that the more embarrassing an event in the gospels the more likely it is to be an accurate portrayal of what happened. These embarrassments had escaped later editors and therefore allow us a brief look at the real history of Jesus. If this argument is followed then it might actually be true that Jesus did not get on well with his family. Yet there is another explanation. Scholars, among them A.N. Wilson, have suggested that Jesus' family troubles might instead reflect a tension in the early church between Gentile followers and the Jewish Christians. These two Christianities had a very different set of belief and practices, as we shall see, and there was enormous debate over whether new converts needed to adhere to the law or not. The Jewish Christians (among them Jesus' very own brother, James the Just) favored a continuation of traditional law but Gentile Christians elsewhere rejected it. So, by depicting Jesus' family as disbelievers who think he is mad the gospel writers are actually trying to distance themselves from the Jewish Christians. They are saying, in effect 'don't believe James and the Jews because they didn't understand Jesus.' Yet there is a strong argument that these first Jewish Christians represented a more authentic version of Jesus' original teaching.

What Happened To Jesus' Brother?

These Jewish sects of Christianity venerated the apocryphal Gospel of the Hebrews above all others. It has been argued that Hebrews was one of the earliest gospels in existence –if not the earliest- and it might have even been written in Aramaic (Jesus' language) rather than the Greek used by the four canonical gospels. The gospel is unfortunately lost, but a few scraps survive as quotations in later books preserved, ironically, by the same men who denounced it as heresy. This alternative gospel was evidently popular and enjoyed a good providence in this period, but it did not fit in with orthodox views centuries later because for one thing Jesus is not divine and Mary wasn't a virgin. It also holds Jesus' brother James in very high regard.

The Ebionites were one such sect of Jewish Christians who are mentioned by the church fathers and who venerated the gospel of the Hebrews. Irenaeus writing towards the end of the second century uses the term 'ebionite' which means the 'poor ones' to describe a sect of Jewish Christians who were stubborn in their clinging to the Jewish law. Irenaeus also says that the Ebionites held James to be the originator of this movement. James then is important to early Jewish sects judging from this evidence, but even within the New Testament there is evidence enough to show that James was the spiritual successor to the movement after the death of Jesus. James appears to be the leader of the Jerusalem church shortly before the city is destroyed by the Roman legions in 70 CE during the First Jewish War.

Paul is a witness to these times and it is among his works that James is revealed to be a man of substance for the fledgling movement. Indeed Paul met with the brother of Jesus:

> "I went up to Jerusalem to get acquainted with Cephas and stayed with him fifteen days. I saw none of the other apostles – only James, the Lord's brother."[37]

We can judge from this that James, the lord's brother, was present at Jerusalem when Paul was writing his letter to the Galatians somewhere around 50 CE.

---

[37] Galatians 1:18-19

Elsewhere Paul portrays James as having some weight among the Jewish Christians.

> *"When Cephas came to Antioch, I opposed him to his face, because he stood condemned. For before certain people came from James, he used to eat with the Gentiles. But when they arrived, he began to draw back and separate himself from the Gentiles because he was afraid of those who belonged to the circumcision group."*[38]

This passage is particularly interesting because we can already see seeds of discontent among the earliest Christian movement. Cephas (better known as Peter) was a Jewish Christian who should have remembered the strict kosher food laws that all Jews had to abide by. By eating with the Gentiles he could quite possibly be in danger of consuming meat that had been sacrificed up on a pagan alter and certainly the animal would not have been killed in the manner proscribed in Mosaic Law. Peter's actions were a clear infringement of this law and he knows he is doing wrong, because when some men came from James he distances himself away from these Gentiles. From this incident we can learn that James had authority in this time, enough to both send men and scare other Jews away from the table. Also we see that James and the men he sends are associated with the 'circumcision group.'

As we before noted, circumcision was a sign of a covenant between the Jews and God so by association we can say that James, brother of Jesus and leader of the Jerusalem Christians, was still a practicing Jew. Paul's argument was that his Gentile followers should not have to be bound by the Jewish laws. Eventually, both sides sat down together to peaceably resolve the issue, or at least that is one side of the story, in actual fact

---

[38] Galatians 2:11-12

there likely was a considerable and heated debate over whether Gentiles would have to go under the knife in order to be considered a follower of Jesus.

In the Book of Acts, at the so-called First Council of Jerusalem, Paul presents his case as to why the Gentiles should not need to be circumcised. Suddenly, without an introduction James gives his verdict on the matter.[39] Perhaps James was powerful and well known enough not to require an introduction but his decision is final and there are no questions or complaints after he has ruled on the matter. Surely James was a man of substance to the first Christian movement.

James was based in Jerusalem outside of the Temple and we can therefore assume that he continued to observe the traditional Jewish purity rites and temple sacrifice that was a feature of Judaism in antiquity. In all respects these first Christians were observant Jews. The only difference between them and other Jews was that the Jewish Christians believed that Jesus was the messiah, while the others were still waiting for the messiah to come.

Josephus describes James' death. Apparently the high priest had accused James of breaking the Jewish laws and had him stoned to death. This, however, was unpopular with the most fair-minded and law obedient people of the city and the priest was removed from his office.[40] James' death has been dated to approximately 62 CE, just a few years before Nero would blame the Christians for the great fire of Rome and eight years before the Temple was obliterated by the Romans. After these events, James' movement disappears from the city although Jewish-Christians will continue to remember him for centuries more.

---

[39] Acts 15:19-21
[40] Antiquities 20.9.1

Interestingly, Jesus' blood relatives do appear many years later and might have even held positions of power within the church. This is based on the evidence of Hegesippus (circa 110-180 CE) who records that *"There still survived of the kindred of the Lord the grandsons of Judas, who according to the flesh was called his brother."* These descendents of Jesus' youngest brother would appear before the Emperor Domitian. Finding no fault with Jesus' grand nephews, the Emperor releases them and they go on to live long lives as leaders of the churches.[41]

In summary, it is possible to see Jesus' blood relatives as having places of honor and importance within the earliest strata of the Christian story and their negative portrayal in the gospels (written largely by Gentiles for Gentiles) is a result of a conflict of interest that was abounding at the time that the gospel writers were compiling their accounts. Should converts be circumcised like James and follow the Jewish law? Or should they remain as they were and accept that belief in Jesus was like a new form of spiritual circumcision as Paul argued? Should they keep the kosher laws or were all foods acceptable? These are just some of the issues that the earliest Christians would have wrestled with. The debate was so fierce that the gospel writers went on to blacken the name of Jesus' family in the gospels so as to make it clear that Christians need not be circumcised.

It was the Jewish Christians, among them James, who preserved a more faithful interpretation of Jesus' original message – Jesus most likely taught a continuation or reinterpretation of the Mosaic Law but it is unlikely that he sought to remove it completely. The winners always write the history and in this case it is

---

[41] Hegesippus, quoted through Eusebius of Caesarea, Historia Ecclesiae, 3:20

the Gentile church that survived. Jesus' family is discredited by the evangelists when they are made to disbelieve Jesus and when they label him as mad.

Conclusions

The gospel writers were adamant to prove Jesus was the messiah and had fulfilled various prophecies - he was born from the line of David and he was born in Bethlehem. Unfortunately, in their attempts to have Jesus born in the right place, Luke and Matthew produce accounts that are wholly inconsistent and in complete contradiction with each other. They have twisted the story of the real Jesus to match with their own expectations and in the end we are left with some very unhistorical stories about the birth of Jesus.

The only way of understanding of Jesus' actual childhood is to study the Galilee from the textual and archaeological evidence and come up with educated guesses about what it must have been like to live in that place in those times, but alas, this is beyond the scope of this book. There is, essentially, a large blank space over Jesus' birth and early life, a space that has been filled by creative evangelists and legendary details, none of which is historical. Things like his virgin birth were not included in the gospels because they are an accurate historical fact, but because they helped the ancients to understand the power of the man they hailed as the messiah.

Most intriguing of all are Jesus' actual siblings, especially James, who continued to teach outside of the temple three decades after his brother's death. We have enough textual evidence about James to recognize him as a practicing Jew, still adhering to elements of the Mosaic Law and holding the reins of the Jerusalem church, and from this we can surmise that Jesus himself must have been a Jew.

CHAPTER FOUR

What Jesus Really Taught

What would you do if you believed that the world was imminently coming to an end? Would you have the same concern with your material possessions as you do now? It is fascinating to think that throughout time there have been periods when communities of people genuinely believed that the end of the world was just around the corner. From ancient times until the present day the enduring belief that the world will one day end continues. There are hundreds of such incidents in recorded history, predictions and preparations are made but as per usual the end never comes. Many of these movements have their roots in Christianity, thanks in part to Jesus' own apocalyptic message that the Kingdom of God would dramatically come.

America in the mid nineteenth century witnessed a common expectation that the end of the world would be within that century. William Miller (1782-1849) was a Baptist preacher from New York State, who during his lifetime was thoroughly convinced that he would live to witness the end of the world. He had calculated the exact date, using an old prophecy in the book of Daniel. Assuming that one-day in the bible was equivalent to one year he came to the horrifying conclusion that the Day of Judgment would be in 1843. He began submitting articles to a Baptist paper which generated a lot of questions from concerned members of the public. His ideas quickly gained in popularity, indeed over half a million copies of the newsletter were distributed in Miller's home state in a mere week. Shorty after his writing, Miller began to preach among congregations of the faithful. What began as a small regional movement quickly found itself with a national audience. Everyone wanted to know exactly when the apocalypse would come but Miller could not nail down the exact time and date, he could only give a rough approximation. It was up to another man to provide the details. Samuel S Snow presented his own calculations at a camp meeting in New Hampshire. Basing his calculations on Miller's, Snow had finally figured that the awaited second coming would happen on 22nd October 1844.

As the date approached, the Millerites, as they were known, were preparing themselves for the end. Thousands of them had given away their properties and possessions expecting to never need them again. After frantic prayers, the date finally arrived. Of course, nothing happened.

"Our fondest hopes and expectations were blasted, and such a spirit of weeping came over us as I never experienced before. It seemed that the loss of all earthly friends could have been no comparison. We wept, and wept, till the day dawn," wrote Hiram Edson, one of the Millerites, reflecting on the desperation and disappointment of the failed prophecy. Some reports show that certain people in the movement then tried to act like children based on the understanding that Jesus had said, *"anyone who will not receive the Kingdom of God like a little child will never enter it."*[42] This bizarre scene serves to demonstrate the passionate and misguided belief these otherwise intelligent people had and the extraordinary extents they went to in order to secure a place for themselves in the afterlife.

After so much hype, Miller and his followers came in for much abuse and mockery. In a letter to a friend, Miller recorded that even children on the street were

---

[42] Mark10:15

mockingly asking people whether they had already purchased a ticket to go on up. One Millerite was even tarred and feathered. The aftermath of the failed apocalypse was known as the Great Disappointment and many followers went back to what was left of their old lives to rebuild what they had so eagerly cast aside. Yet Miller had planted a seed of thought in the fertile minds of these congregations and from these roots emerged the Seventh Day Adventist church, which is still very much active in the world today.

By the mid nineteenth century a belief in the end times was nothing new. Indeed it was a feature too of Judaism in the time of Jesus, and by all indications Jesus himself taught a similar message to the Millerites - repent, for the end is nigh.

How Did Jesus Teach?

As we have seen not much is known about Jesus after his birth in a small and inconsequential village in the rural province of Galilee. He next appears beside the banks of the river Jordon, according to Luke in the fifteenth year of the rein of Tiberius, or approximately 29 CE. By Luke's reckoning Jesus was thirty years old by this time. At the Jordan he meets John the Baptist. John calls for the repentance of the people and immerses them in the river water once they have repented their sins. Josephus describes John as a good man, who calls the Jews to practice righteousness and piety to God, and in his day John was an extremely popular figure. He is so popular that the gospels cannot ignore him, but instead frame his mission as a precursor to that of Jesus'. After Jesus is immersed in the water by John the voice of God proclaims *"This is my Son, whom I love; with him I am well pleased."*[43]

---

[43] Matthew 3:17

After his baptism, the synoptics tell us that Jesus enters the bleak desert for forty days where he is tempted by the devil. Although Jesus' meeting the devil is legendary, the wandering in the desert is traditionally a Jewish way of finding closeness with God. At any rate, Jesus escapes unscathed and immediately recruits some disciples to assist him in his mission. Mark tells us that he found the first four beside the Sea of Galilee and promised to make them fishers of men. They drop everything to follow Jesus.

Jesus next wanders the lands around Galilee visiting towns such as Capernaum and the various villages scattered around the province. He does return to Nazareth but the people there reject him. What is interesting is that the gospels never portray Jesus visiting any of the larger urban settlements. Sepphoris and Scythopolis were the biggest cities closest to Nazareth but Jesus appears to avoid them all together. Jesus does go to Tiberias but only to the outskirts of the city and not to the center. We cannot know for sure the reasons why Jesus does this. Since the citizens of the cities would have been richer than the outlying villages was Jesus weary of the corrupting influence of money? Or was he instead cautious of the foreigners who lived in these cities? Scythopolis in the province of Samaria was only twenty miles or so from Nazareth but it was a very Hellenized city that had come under direct Roman control in 64 BCE. The gospels do contain hints that Jesus framed his mission only to the 'lost sheep of Israel' and not to the Gentiles so this is a possibility.

Jesus reaches out to the poorer sections of society but also to the sinners. He appears quite comfortable in the company of the tax collectors and the women of lesser virtue. Indeed it was his idea that the last would be the first to enter the Kingdom of God, a message that appealed to many, but certainly would have shocked the few who were at the top of Jewish society.

Jesus evidently found popular appeal. Many came out from the towns and villages to hear him speak, and some began to follow him. All of the gospels are quite clear that Jesus attracted much attention. The story of the feeding of five thousand people who had assembled to listen to Jesus speak, although exaggerated, serves to show that there were substantial crowds following him. Another incident has Jesus having to be lowered into a house from the roof because he could not enter the door for all the crowds waiting to see him. However, not everyone is pleased to hear Jesus' teaching. Among his enemies were the Pharisees who accuse Jesus of fragrantly breaking the Mosaic Law and they begin to plot to kill him. This will culminate a few years later in Jerusalem in his death. Or at least this is what the gospels say, the truth of the matter will be explored later.

This is the briefest of sketches of how Jesus taught that will give us a context as we examine in greater detail the content of Jesus' teaching. The point here is to show that Jesus did have a mission and he did have a popular following. That the gospels depict a great many crowds attracted to Jesus surely illustrates that his message was essentially Jewish in nature. If it had been otherwise none of the Jews would have followed him.

Was Jesus Really A Jew?

It has often been remarked that Jesus was a Jew. This is a simple statement and one that would appear to be true of the historical Jesus. Jesus was born in the Jewish village of Nazareth and as a child his parents would have presented him to the Temple and Jesus would have been circumcised according to the law, as we noted earlier. Even his name, which in its original form was 'Yeshua,' was an exceedingly popular name for

Jewish children in those times and indeed the Old Testament is filled with many other Yeshuas.

Furthermore, despite all of the polishing that the story of Jesus has suffered at the hands of the evangelists who want to promote their own version of Jesus, in places his essential Jewishness is so firmly ingrained that it cannot easily be done away with. Thus we are reminded of Matthew's statement that Jesus had not come to abolish the law but to fulfill it and further Jesus' appeal to his followers to be as righteous as the Pharisees themselves.[44]

Most revealing is an incident in which Jesus heals a leper. The afflicted man begs of Jesus *"If you are willing you can make me clean."* Jesus miraculously heals the man and then instructs him to *"Show yourself to the priest and offer the sacrifices that Moses commanded for your cleansing."*[45] This cleansing at the Temple was a commandment from God as specified in the Book of Leviticus:

> *"If the person has been healed of his infectious skin disease, the priest shall order that two live clean birds and some cedar wood, scarlet yarn and hyssop be brought for the one to be cleansed. Then the priest shall order that one of the birds be killed over fresh water in a clay pot. He is then to take the live bird and dip it, together with the cedar wood, the scarlet yarn and the hyssop, into the blood of the bird that was killed over the fresh water. Seven times he shall sprinkle the one to be cleansed of the infectious disease and pronounce him clean. Then he is to release the live bird in the open fields."*[46]

That is just the first stage really since the poor leper must shave off his hair – all of it including his eyebrows - wash

---

[44] See Matthew 5:17-20

[45] Mark 1:40-44

[46] Leviticus 14:3-6

himself and his clothes, live outside his tent for a week, and then come back for another round of animal slaughter. The law was commonly observed in Jesus' time and it is not therefore farfetched to suggest that Jesus might have commanded such a ritual to be observed. This story passes the criteria for embarrassment (it conflicted with later church teaching and therefore was more likely to be true) and it fits in with what a first century Jewish Rabbi might tell a leper to do. Jesus as a Jew would have understood the law to be commandments from God and therefore unbreakable. He likely strove to interpret it but to say that he sought to remove it is wrong.

There are other references to Jesus' Jewish nature. Luke states that *"Each day Jesus was teaching at the temple."*[47] It is hard to conceive why he would teach there if he did not have a Jewish message. Indeed we shall shortly learn that the primary content of Jesus' teaching was in line with the Judaism of his time and the fact that he was labeled as the messiah serves only to demonstrate Jesus' fundamental Jewishness – the messiah was a very Jewish idea. Jesus is constantly hailed as 'rabbi' by those who meet him. Since 'Rabbi' means simply a teacher we must ask what was Jesus teaching if it were not the interpretation of the law and the Jewish scriptures which he was evidently very familiar with. When for example Jesus is wandering in the desert he is able to respond to Satan's temptations by quoting examples taken directly out of these ancient texts.

Here we shall examine two very different aspects of Jesus, his clothing and his relationship with the Pharisees in order to demonstrate that Jesus was indeed

---

[47] Luke 21:37

a Jew but also to help us envisage how the historical Jesus might have looked as he roamed the Galilee.

What Did Jesus Wear?

There are no physical descriptions of Jesus anywhere in the New Testament however his clothing is indirectly hinted at in a couple of passages. The Jews, especially pious ones, had their clothing dictated to them by God. There is an example of a commandment made in the Book of Numbers for the Jews to make for themselves fringes on their garments so that they will remember God.[48] The book of Deuteronomy is also clear on the subject: *"You shall make tassels on the four corners of the clothing with which you cover [yourself]."*[49] These tassels are known as 'Tzitzit' and are still in use by practitioners of Judaism today. Use of these tassels is old, possibly dating back to the eight century BCE, and they certainly would have been in use in Jesus' time.

Now compare God's commandments with what is written in the gospels: *"Now a woman, having a flow of blood for twelve years, who had spent all her livelihood on physicians and could not be healed by any, came from behind and touched the border of His [Jesus'] garment. And immediately her flow of blood stopped."*[50] The term 'border' is in fact the translation of the tzitzit specified in the Old Testament. That Jesus is depicted as wearing them is hardly a surprise since he was a Jewish rabbi.

Tassels weren't the only uniquely Jewish garment that Jesus would have worn. Another commandment of God was to wear passages of the Torah upon the body. This is commanded in both the books of Exodus and Deuteronomy, and indeed archaeological evidence from

---

[48] See Numbers 15:38-39
[49] Deuteronomy 22:12
[50] Luke 8:43-44

the site of the Dead Sea Scrolls has confirmed that such things were used by Jews of Jesus' era. Today practicing Jews fasten little boxes to their arms and forehead in remembrance of this commandment. They are known in Greek as 'phylacteries.' Jesus makes a comment on them and the tzitzit in Matthew when criticizing the hypocritical Pharisees: *"They do all their deeds to be seen by others; for they make their phylacteries broad and their fringes long."*[51]

Jesus appears to be criticizing the Pharisees because they like to advertise the fact that they are observant Jews. He is not criticizing them for wearing the boxes or the tassels since that commandment came from God and the Pharisees were only following the law. The point here is that Jesus was appalled that they wore extra large boxes and fringes simply to show off. Nowhere in the gospels does Jesus say that these items of clothing are now redundant and so it would not be farfetched to suggest that Jesus himself wore similar clothing, although to small specifications.

Why Does Jesus Fight With The Pharisees?

Jesus' arguments with the Pharisees extend to everything; they reject sinners while Jesus embraces them. Jesus hates their man made rules (a reference to the oral law and the Pharisees' own traditions) and instead he wants people to find a closer relationship with God. The portrayal of this sect of Judaism is negative throughout the gospels. Despite this, some scholars have posited that Jesus might have been a Pharisee himself. It is true from a look at later rabbinic writing that the Jews regularly argued amongst themselves in order to find the correct way of

---

[51] Matthew 23:5

interpreting the law and Jesus debating the size of the phylacteries fits snugly with this image.

All Jews agreed that there is one God and that through his prophet Moses the law was given. Other than this there was no official dogma, no codified Jewish bible and religious practice was varied and open to interpretation. When Jesus is shown to be opposed to the Pharisees in actuality he was debating the best way to interpret the law, much as many a rabbi has done since.

Despite Jesus giving the Pharisees a lampooning for their overreliance on things like ritual purity, elsewhere his message is remarkably similar to theirs. Both Jesus and the Pharisees share a common enmity against the Sadducees, the ruling elite of Jerusalem, and both Jesus and the Pharisees share a belief that the dead could rise – something the Sadducees fundamentally oppose. It is often the case that we fight fiercely with the ones closest to us. Thinking like this has led some to wonder if Jesus was also a Pharisee.

Taking this line of thought further; some scholars have not merely identified Jesus as being a Pharisee, but more specifically being of the school of Hillel. Hillel (circa 110 BCE - 10 BCE) was a famous Jewish sage and scholar living in Jerusalem at the time of Herod the Great and was held in high regard by the Pharisees, and indeed by many Jews of his age. He founded a movement called the House of Hillel which was known for its debates with its opposing faction, the Beit Shammai, concerning the correct interpretation of the law. Although these disputes were often harsh, evidence from the Talmud shows that there was some intermarriage between the two groups. Far from being blood enemies these factions were actually striving for the same thing – correct interpretation of the Mosaic

Law. Jesus arguing with the Pharisees could easily be seen in a similar vein.

Anyway, Hillel's influence was great indeed and his dynasty lasted many years after his death. He was most famous for his golden rule: *"What is hateful to you, do not do to your fellow: this is the whole Torah; the rest is the explanation; go and learn."*[52] This sentiment can also be heard in Jesus own words. Compare Jesus' statement in Matthew to that of Hillel's golden rule: *"So in everything, do to others what you would have them do to you, for this sums up the Law and the Prophets."*[53] Certainly these are very similar in wording and the same in sentiment, both urge the Jews to be mindful of others and both assert that this is the summary of the entire Torah.

Of course, we can never know whether proponents of this view are right in pronouncing Jesus a student of the school of Hillel but for sure Hillel was very important in his time and his teaching extended into Jesus' own. Jesus could easily have found inspiration in them, even if he was not a Pharisee nor of Hillel's school. Whether or not Jesus was a Pharisee is not really the point of this discussion. Instead it serves to illustrate beyond doubt that Jesus was a Jew. But if Jesus is a law interpreting Jew why then do the gospels have the Pharisees as the chief protagonists in much of Jesus' story? Why do they plot to kill Jesus over his alleged law breaking?

The gospel authors were compiling their accounts of Jesus outside of the original Jewish context and were seeking to distance themselves from the Jews in their own time. For example, the Gentile Mark might have been writing his gospel during or shortly after the Jewish War when zealous Jews fought against the might

---

[52] Mishnah, Shabbat 31a
[53] Matthew 7.12

of Rome. He was keen to show Christianity was a safe religion and compatible with Rome and he blames the Jews for killing Jesus, while at the same time exonerating the Romans from the crime.

The Pharisees would survive the traumatic series of rebellions and would flourish into the Judaism as we know it today. Throughout the Christian period many observant Jews would be followers of the Pharisee movement who rejected the evangelist's claims that Jesus was the messiah. Perhaps this is why their name is so thoroughly blackened in the gospels, just as Jesus' family is discredited.

Christians have often interpreted Jesus' fighting with the Pharisees as an indication that he essentially disagreed with their observance of the Mosaic Law. This proposition has more to do with the attitudes in the later Christian churches that were opposed to the law and had discontinued its practice. According to their idea, Jesus had cleared away the old laws and represented something new.

The most credible view is that the historical Jesus still observed and interpreted the law, as did most Jews. In fact, the gospels don't contain a single incident of Jesus breaking the law or recommending others to contravene it. For example, when the followers of Jesus pluck grain on a Sabbath (when no work was allowed according to the law) the Pharisees complain that their actions are unlawful.[54] However, it is Jesus' followers who picked the grain and not Jesus. Furthermore, Jesus' response is to offer an interpretation based on the scriptures as to why it is permissible for his followers to pick the grain, he gives the example of David entering the house of

---

[54] See Mark 2:23-24

God to eat consecrated bread. Here Jesus is interpreting the law and not breaking it.

Did Jesus Believe The End of The World Was Near?

"The time has come," Jesus says in Mark's gospel. *"The Kingdom of God is near. Repent and believe the good news!"*[55] This seems to summarize his mission as portrayed in the synoptic gospels, although Matthew calls it the 'Kingdom of Heaven' because as a Jew he would have been cautious about using the sacred name of God. To deduce what this kingdom was we must first reflect back on some elements of Jewish belief.

There was a prevailing thought among many Jews that they were living in evil times. Before Jesus' birth, King Herod was regarded as being a part of this earthly injustice - he had flagrantly abused his power, he removed the justified line of the Hasmonean priests away from the temple and had allowed pagan shrines to be built for example in and around Caesarea. He was also responsible for killing righteous men such as John the Baptist. After Herod's death, his Roman allies took over direct control of Judea and once again foreign pagans would rule over God's chosen race. It must have seemed that everything the Hasmoneans had achieved was steadily being unwound. The Romans understood little of the Jewish sensibilities, as when the Emperor Nero decided to erect a statue of himself in the temple. This was intolerable to observant Jews and would have reminded them of the historical events preceding the Maccabean Revolt.

Many Jews thought that their suffering would be alleviated somehow. Indeed God had always redeemed his chosen people; he had taken them out of slavery in Egypt, he had taken them out of exile in Babylon, he

---

[55] Mark 1:16

had given them the Maccabees and surely he would do something now.

There were, of course, prophecies that an ancestor of David would rise to redeem Israel and would re-unite the twelve tribes of Israel. The message of the historical Jesus is unmistakably tied in with the redemption of Israel. From all of the gospels, and from Paul, we learn that Jesus had exactly twelve disciples. This is a highly symbolic number indicative of Jesus' expectation that God would intervene to reunite the twelve tribes and as a consequence restore Israel to its former glory. Certainly this idea is present in the gospels, for example in Matthew: *"I tell you the truth, at the renewal of all things, when the Son of Man sits on his glorious throne, you who have followed me will also sit on twelve thrones, judging the twelve tribes of Israel."*[56] If Jesus really had said this, then it is evident that he saw himself in a rather elevated light, but certainly the Jewish author of Matthew understood the terms 'messiah' 'son of David' and 'the kingdom of God' as pointing towards Israel's redemption. Matthew frames his narrative of Jesus within an overarching theme of redemption and his attempts to parallel the life of Jesus with that of Moses are most revealing of all. Moses was God's tool of redemption and to Matthew's eye so too was Jesus.

If Jesus assumed the kingdom would restore Israel then this was a very political teaching, at least as far as the Romans would have understood it. All the talk of kingdoms and a renewed Israel would be alarming to the Roman rulers who were asserting their own imperial dominance in the region. And if among Jesus' disciples there really was a man named Judas Iscariot (the dagger man) and Simeon the Zealot (the rebel),

---

[56] Matthew 19:28

Jesus suddenly takes on the appearance of a revolutionary and political rebel opposed to Roman imperial rule, as some historians have posited.

Besides the political situation, the world was one full of misery and pain. Disease, demons and death prevailed. Since the Jews believed that God was watching over everything many would have asked - where was the divine justice in all of this? Surely there would come a time when the Israelites would be alleviated of their suffering. A time when there is no disease, no death, but also a time when Israel was once again redeemed. The Kingdom of God was also understood by some Jews to be a remedy for these issues, but what exactly do the gospels expect the Kingdom of God to be?

There is no exact definition of what form the Kingdom would take but there are enough clues to re-construct what the gospel writers thought it to be. The Lord's Prayer as recorded in Matthew sheds some light on the matter, it says *"your kingdom come, your will be done on earth as it is in heaven."*[57] From this the Kingdom appears to be a period of time when God's rule would descend to the earth. Presumably, God's rule in the heavens was just and once it had arrived there would be heavenly justice on the earth.

To enter the kingdom one should therefore act in a just manner and without sin: *"And if your eye causes you to sin, pluck it out. It is better for you to enter the Kingdom of God with one eye than to have two eyes and be thrown into hell."*[58] This statement shows that the kingdom was something that could be entered into through righteous behavior. It is these concerns on how to enter the kingdom that preoccupy much of Jesus' teachings.

---

[57] Matthew 6:10
[58] Mark 9:47

Originally, the Jewish concept of the Kingdom of God was of an event that would take place in the future time, but in the present space. Thus many Jews of the age were expecting a calamity of catastrophic proportions that would redeem Israel in this physical reality (as distinguished from a spiritual one in the afterlife). The Qumran community was expecting a very real event like this to occur. They expected the earthly rulers to be knocked down and replaced by justified and pious rulers, who happened to be themselves. Although this event would occur in this physical realm it would be accompanied by all kinds of supernatural phenomenon.

We can get a flavor of what the first Christians thought the Kingdom would bring from a read of the gospels. When Jesus is questioned by his disciples about this event, he describes a whole series of calamities that would precede the kingdom. Many would be led astray, there would be wars, earthquakes and famines but this is simply the beginning of the end. False Christs and false prophets would emerge promising to perform wonderful deeds. Finally, Mark's Jesus describes what that day will look like:

> "the sun will be darkened, and the moon will not give its light; the stars will fall from the sky, and the heavenly bodies will be shaken."[59]

Like the Qumran community there was an expectation that the messiah would arise to herald these times.

Paul wrote about his understanding of the kingdom independently of the gospels but there are remarkable similarities. To illustrate this one need merely regard Paul's statement about the Kingdom alongside Matthew's:

> "the Lord himself will come down from heaven, with a loud command, with the voice of the archangel and

---

[59] Mark 13:24 Quoting Isaiah 13:10

with the trumpet call of God, and the dead in Christ will rise first. After that, we who are still alive and are left will be caught up together with them in the clouds to meet the Lord in the air. And so we will be with the Lord forever." [60]

Compared to Matthew:

"At that time the sign of the Son of Man will appear in the sky, and all the nations of the earth will mourn. They will see the Son of Man coming on the clouds of the sky, with power and great glory. And he will send his angels with a loud trumpet call, and they will gather his elect from the four winds, from one end of the heavens to the other."[61]

Both these independent sources mention a heavenly figure appearing among the clouds of the sky followed by angelic trumpet calls and the elect, or those still alive, will meet the Lord. The Kingdom of God is so strongly attested in the gospels and so firmly rooted in Jewish thought that we can safely say that Jesus was expecting God to intervene in the affairs of the Jews.

This wasn't a lazy prediction of events that would occur thousands of years in the future, the Kingdom was coming very soon indeed: Jesus tells his audience, *"I tell you the truth, some who are standing here will not taste death before they see the Son of Man coming in his kingdom."*[62] The literal interpretation of this statement is that the kingdom is so close at hand that some among Jesus' closest followers will still be alive when it happens. This suggests a period of months or even years - the Kingdom is painfully close!

---

[60] 1 Thessalonians 4:16-17
[61] Matthew 24:30-31
[62] Matthew 16:28

This sense of a terrific, terrible and very imminent event is so powerful that it transcends Jesus' original context and is a central theme of Paul also. *"According to the Lord's own word, we tell you that we who are still alive, who are left till the coming of the Lord, will certainly not precede those who have fallen asleep."*[63] Paul's motivation for writing his letter to the Thessalonians (the earliest Christian writing composed just two decades after Jesus' death), in modern day Greece, is to reassure the community of Christians burgeoning there. They too were watching the skies for the coming Kingdom and expect it to happen at any moment. The problem is that some of their members had already died (Paul says they are asleep because he believes they will reawaken at the resurrection). The Thessalonian church is fearful over their deceased brethren and is writing to Paul to ask whether those who were dead would be missing out, had they died too soon to expect a rebirth? No, is Paul's happy answer. The faithful at Thessalonica need not mourn like other men for the Kingdom will reach even those who had fallen asleep.

In another of Paul's letters, his first epistle to the church that he founded in Corinth, we can see additional evidence that he believed the end times were fast approaching. He is writing to answer various points that have cropped up regarding the behavior of his converts there. Among them is some advice on marriage. Since Paul believes that *'the time is short'* what then should the believers do? Should they get married or not? Paul's solution is this *"because of the current crisis, I think that is good for you to remain as you are. Are you married? Do not seek a divorce. Are you unmarried? Do not look for a wife."*[64] Since time is short and the *'world in its*

---

[63] 1 Thessalonians 15
[64] 1 Corinthians 27

present form is passing away' it is better for the followers to concentrate on pleasing the Lord than be distracted by worldly affairs such as divorce and marriage.

A drastic expectation that God would interfere with world affairs and redeem the nation of Israel is thus found in the Dead Sea Scrolls, the gospels and the writings of Paul. These three distinct lines of evidence make it highly likely that Jesus the Jew expected the end very soon.

Was Jesus A Failed Prophet?

Jesus, therefore, can quite plausibly be regarded as expecting an extremely imminent event that would be witnessed by some who were still alive within his own lifetime. However, the church soon found itself rather embarrassed by these predictions because put quite simply, the end never came!

Usually, whenever an ancient source attributes an historical event to the fulfillment of prophecy the historian is cautious, especially when the prophecy and event match each other exactly. This smacks of later hindsight by the author. This is not the case with Jesus' prediction of the Kingdom of God, however, because the prophecy and the event are completely discordant. So far there have been no falling stars, no angels blowing trumpets and certainly no dead rising from their graves. The Kingdom of God in its literal sense, the sense understood by Jesus, Paul and the first Christians, did not arrive within their lifetimes. Jesus, it seems, has issued a failed prophecy.

This is clearly a problem that later generations of Christians had to deal with. How could Jesus be the Son of God and the messiah when his own prophecies did not come true? Thankfully, Christians are able to creatively work out problems like these by assuming that Jesus was talking metaphorically or that the disciples had misunderstood an important aspect of the teaching. To skeptics this seems like an easy cop out clause.

In the Second Epistle of Peter, composed by an anonymous author in the name of Peter around 100-150 CE, people are evidently still wondering why the Kingdom hadn't come seventy years after Jesus had died. The response in the epistle is revealing. *"First of all, you must understand that in the last days scoffers will come, scoffing and following their own evil desires. They will say, 'Where is this 'coming' he promised? Ever since our fathers died, everything goes on as it has since the beginning of creation.'"*[65] To solve this problem, the author of Peter reminds them that to God one day can seem like a thousand years and thus escapes embarrassment. It is a neat explanation but one that twists Jesus' original sentiment. Today, Christians have a slightly different response; the Kingdom has already come but it is a spiritual place and not an actual Kingdom that would physically re-order the world. Jesus' prediction was actually a reminder for mankind to reform itself and one should live their life as if the Kingdom was just around the corner. In other words Jesus' predictions were symbolic.

It is interesting to observe that the further away in time we are from Jesus, the less literal is the understanding of the Kingdom in Christian thought. This is an adaptation of the original prophecies, but still does not escape the fact that the ancients were expecting a very literal, very imminent change to the existing world order which did not happen.

---

[65] 2 Peter 3:3-9

How Should We Follow Jesus?

As you might expect from a group of zealous Jews who foresaw that the end of the world was very close the first believers, like the Millerites, did not see the point of worldly goods. Riches were rejected because it was more important to spread the good news than to be concerned with wealth. When Jesus, in Luke, is preparing to send out the disciples to preach about the Kingdom of God and heal the sick, *"He told them: 'Take nothing for the journey –no staff, no bag, no bread, no money, no extra tunic."*[66] Jesus it seems is not a fan of accumulating physical possessions and from this description we can imagine a bunch of men travelling through the lands proclaiming Jesus' message but living very humbly.

Perhaps Jesus' own background does play a part in his rejection of wealth, he was after all a Galilean, a land of fishermen and farmers. That he is against the rich is evidently clear in the gospels. *"But woe to you who are rich, for you have already received your comfort"*[67] seems to sum up Jesus' opinion of the wealthy. In Mark, a rich young man approaches Jesus and kneels before him, he asks *"what must I do to inherit eternal life?"* Jesus reminds the man of God's commandments in a rather impatient manner to which the boy declares *"all these I have kept since I was a boy."* Jesus tells him that he is lacking something, *"go, sell everything you have and give to the poor, and you will have treasure in heaven. Then come, follow me."*[68] His answer doesn't please the boy since he is already rich and he turns away disappointed. It is interesting that Mark agrees with Luke that disciples should leave behind everything in order to follow Jesus.

---

[66] Luke 9:3
[67] Luke 6:24
[68] Mark 10:17

"We have left behind everything to follow you!" Peter complains. What they have left behind is clarified in Jesus' response. *"No one who has left home or brothers or sisters or mother or father or children or fields for me and the gospel will fail to receive a hundred times as much in this present age...and in the age to come, eternal life."*[69] The point is simple, leave behind everything and proclaim the gospel in order to achieve everlasting life. One disciple really wants to follow Jesus but begs Jesus *"Lord, first let me go and bury my father,"* but Jesus refuses to allow him, saying *"Follow me, and let the dead bury their own dead."*[70]

This fact may be uncomfortable for many well-to-do Christians today, but Jesus' rejection of wealth and possessions and his demands that his followers give up everything is historically credible. We do see a precedent for just this kind of thing in the Qumran Community. Archaeological excavations at Qumran and an analysis of the texts which they maintained, as well as a review of what Josephus has to tell us about the Essenes, reveals that among first century Jews there was a practice of rejecting material wealth in order to better reach God. And we should not forget the example of John the Baptist who lived in a cave, wore a simple dress of camel hair and ate nothing but locusts and honey. All of this evidence provides the historian with a strong base for supposing that the historical Jesus did continue to practice voluntary poverty. Therefore, we can say that Jesus is acting within the context of first century Judaism when he disavows worldly goods. Furthermore, voluntary poverty is a feature of the Jewish Christians. The sect that revered James for example was called the Ebionites which means the 'poor ones'.

---

[69] Mark 10:29-31
[70] Matthew 8:21-22

In the Book of Acts we learn that Barnabas sold his own land and donated the proceeds to the apostles who then handed the money to the poor.[71] Perhaps, Barnabas was aware of Jesus' parable of the rich man and had sold everything he owned in order to find for himself a place in the Kingdom. Indeed this teaching is so well attested that it is highly likely that Jesus himself taught these things.

Many Christians today go about their daily lives, heading to work and then returning home to their families, but according to Jesus if they truly want to enter the Kingdom then shouldn't they give up all of this?

Was Jesus The Messiah?

The Kingdom of God was understood to be at hand and there was the Jewish belief that the messiah would precede it. The gospels unswervingly portray Jesus as the Christ (Christ being the same as the messiah). There are continual references to prophecies in the Old Testament which we are meant to take as evidence that Jesus fulfilled them and was therefore the messiah. Yet the gospels were written years after Jesus' death and the evangelists who wrote them were often content to bend Jesus' story to match these prophecies – thus we end up with Jesus riding on two donkeys and rather shaky 'evidence' of Jesus' bloodline. Just because the gospel writers want us to believe that Jesus is the awaited one it doesn't necessarily follow that Jesus himself ever said he was and so we are justified in asking whether it is conceivable that Jesus ever thought of himself as the messiah.

To answer this question we must first try to understand what exactly the term 'messiah' really means, but this is not an easy proposition. Before Christians start

---

[71] See Acts 4:36-37

proclaiming Jesus to be the messiah there was in fact no definite understanding of what the title represents in any Jewish text. There is no text for example which specifically lists all of the qualities expected of the messiah. The term messiah itself means 'anointed,' which suggests a religious or kingly role because in the Old Testament priests, prophets and kings are all described as being anointed. Typically, oil was poured over the head of the anointed which signified his ordination in the above-mentioned roles. The Jews understood that 'the anointed one' was to be blessed by God for his role.

Assuming for a minute that Jesus really did conceive of himself as a messiah, or as one who was anointed, he could then have envisaged himself as some kind of prophet or king. Certainly, the gospels believe that Jesus was executed as 'king of the Jews' as his epitaph on the cross read. If Jesus had seen himself in a kingly role this might explain why Pontius Pilate had him killed – the Romans would be extremely vigilant of men proclaiming their kingly status as it was a challenge to their own authority in Judea. We cannot know for certain whether Jesus really thought this or not, although the evangelists have made their opinions clear. The one clear cut piece of evidence that is beyond dispute is the fact that Jesus had exactly twelve disciples which represented the reunited twelve tribes of Israel. If Jesus was their leader then this may provide a clue as to how he envisaged his own role; as a kingly figure.

Since Christians argue that Jesus is the messiah predicted in the Jewish scriptures we should hence examine further the Jewish conceptualization of the messiah. There is not much material in the Jewish texts that reveal what the prophesized messiah would be like. Having said that, there are at least two examples that can shed some light on the subject. The community who gave us the Dead Sea Scrolls was envisaging a future event involving not one, but two messiahs. The appearance of a son of Aaron and a son of David would signify a great war which would see angelic armies defeating the forces of evil. Another source of information are the Psalms of Solomon, which are referred to in Christian literature but are not canonical, nor are they canonical in the Jewish scriptures. Written in the era of 40-70 BCE the Psalms seem to refer to the invasion of the Roman general Pompey but they are definitely expecting a catastrophic event associated with a messiah-like figure:

> *"Behold, O Lord, and raise up unto them their king, the son of David, at the time known to you, O God, in order that he may reign over Israel your servant. And gird him with strength, that he may shatter unrighteous rulers, and that he may purge Jerusalem from Gentiles who trample her down to destruction."*[72]

From the Dead Sea scrolls and the Psalms of Solomon, we see a hope that God would keep his promise to David and raise one of his ancestors for the sake of Israel's redemption. According to the Psalms of Solomon, the son of David is a military ruler and in connection with this the Dead Sea Scrolls foresaw a war with heavenly as well as human armies. Thus the messiah was envisaged to have a military function. By these standards the Christian version of the messiah, the savior of humanity, does not accord with the little textual evidence we have. Certainly the gospel writers fully believed that Jesus was the son of David and went to extraordinary lengths to shape their gospels accordingly and therefore we must conclude that much

---

[72] Psalms of Solomon 17:21-22

of the Christian claims are a re-invention of the term to suit their own theology. This was not a deceitful maneuver because the evangelists really did believe Jesus was special in some way, and by showing that Jesus was the product of an ancient prophecy many more Gentiles converts would have been made.

Messianic claimants are quite numerous throughout history. A recent one was Menachem Mendel Schneerson (1902-1994) who led a sect of orthodox Jews and was hailed as the messiah by some of his followers. Indeed, history is littered with would-be messiahs. Even Simon Bar Kokhba the leader of the Jewish uprising against the Romans in 132–136 CE was also labeled as the messiah by his followers. When his uprising failed the case for his messiahship was quickly dropped. Both these examples illustrate that within Judaism, then and now, there was nothing problematic or contradictory to Judaism in hailing someone as the messiah. Great military deeds or even powerful teaching have been used as evidence of messianic status through the ages. There is nothing inherently blasphemous in making these claims either - the messiah was understood to be a man who was favored by God, which does not contravene Judaism's strict monotheism. Conceivably then, Jesus might have roamed the lands believing he was a messiah of some variety or other, but naturally this was not the divine messiah envisaged by the Christians years later.

The fact that the earliest sects of Christians, both Jewish and Gentile, held Jesus to be the messiah would indicate that this was a feature of the earliest movement's belief. Paul believes it, the gospels writers believe it so it is therefore quite likely that either Jesus called himself messiah during his lifetime or at least some of his followers proclaimed him so shortly after his death. As we noted, there was an expectation that the messiah would precede a magnificent event that would see the redemption of Israel. As Jesus was warning his fellow Jews about the immanency of the Kingdom, he conceivably could have understood himself to have been the messiah, but when years later the Kingdom had yet to arrive the figure of Jesus and his teaching was adapted.

Did Jesus Say That He Was The Son of God?

Jesus several times in the gospels speaks of himself or is referred to as the 'Son of God.' The mistake that many Christians make is to take the term on its literal meaning: that God had at one time felt the need for a son and that the son was Jesus. In this view, Jesus shared the substance of God and was an aspect of the creator being, so when Jesus could suspend the laws of nature through his miracle working he was able to do so because he was essentially God in human form. These ideas derive from the later Christian teaching. We know that Jesus would never have conceived of himself as a God because he was very much a Jew of his age, and all Jews of this age were strict monotheists. The idea of a man being God was repulsive to Jews as their refusal to offer sacrifices to the Roman Emperors indicates. So what does the title 'Son of God' actually mean?

Once again we must examine the original Jewish context of this title to properly understand it and determine whether it was a title that Jesus might have applied to himself. Throughout the Old Testament, the term 'Son of God' was applied to many different people who all enjoyed a unique and close relationship with God. *"When Israel was a child, I loved him, and out of Egypt I called my son,"*[73] are Yahweh's words regarding his

---

[73] Hosea 11:1

chosen race of people, the Israelites. In fact, throughout the Old Testament the 'Son of God' or 'sons of God' refer specifically to three things: Israel and its people, heavenly beings such as angels and the kings of Israel.

In a sense, anyone who was faithful to the law and who revered God above all else could be regarded as a son of God. The performance of good deeds and a strong faith in God could also lead to a Jew being described in this way. This conclusion is supported by other Jewish writings, particularly in later rabbinic literature. Jesus Ben Sira (writing 175-180 BCE) calls for his people to care for others and in return *"god shall call you son, and shall have mercy on you."* Jesus as a Jew, a holy man, a righteous teacher and a man learned in law was in this respect a son of God. In its original Jewish setting this title had nothing to do with a man's divinity.

Christians have taken the title out of its original Jewish context and understood it to be indicative of Jesus' greater status as an aspect of God himself. In actual fact there is no precedence for a wholly divine messiah in any Jewish writings. However, to later generations of Gentile Christians who had less understanding of the intricacies of Jewish scriptures, this term meant something else entirely. When hearing that Jesus was the Son of God, the first Roman converts would have fallen back on their own cultural background which was much more permissive to the notion that a man could attain divine status. Julius Caesar (100-44 BCE) for example was officially declared to be a divinity by the Senate, and his heir Augustus (64 BCE-14 CE) produced coins for propaganda purposes inscribed with the words *'if father is divine, so is the son.'* Even further back in time we see men who laid a claim of divinity. When Alexander the Great (356–323 BCE) marched into Egypt he was proclaimed as the son of Amun, the king of the

Egyptian gods, by an oracle and from then on he regarded himself as such. With these ideas being a feature of Greco-Roman culture it is not hard to image how the title 'son of god' was interpreted differently from its original Jewish context.

Yes, Jesus conceivably might have called himself 'Son of God' but in doing so was affirming his close relationship with God as a humble and human servant. As a first century Jew he could not have said 'I am god.' The Jews were, and are, strict monotheists and the punishment for blasphemy back then was beheading.

The 'Son of Man' is yet another title in the New Testament which like the Son of God has matured away from its original Jewish context. In the Christian understanding, the Son of Man is Jesus, the messiah, the Son of God. The gospels seem to have two distinct meanings of the title, the first of which is a heavenly entity who will descend to earth to create a new world order. *"At that time men will see the Son of Man coming in clouds with great power and glory."*[74] The second usage is by Jesus when referring to himself. The assumption is that Jesus was to be this heavenly figure who would ride the clouds, but this is a fallacy. After stating he is the Son of Man no one questions Jesus as to its meaning, which would have been extraordinary if Jesus had really thought that he would return on a cloud – he was talking to Jews most of the time, and their interest would certainly have been piqued if Jesus was referring to himself as this divine entity. What does 'Son of Man' mean then?

The problem with all the Jewish titles (Son of God, Son of Man and the Messiah) is that there are no concrete definitions in any of the scriptures. Originally, the Son

---

[74] Mark 13:26-27

of Man appears to be a mere personal pronoun, that is, a more formal way of saying 'I'. The best example of this is the Prophet Ezekiel who frequently referred to himself as the Son of Man. In the Jewish interpretation this title is indicative of human weakness and fragility, and indeed some Christians have understood this title to indicate the human side of Jesus.

However, it is confusing to have the Son of Man as both a divine being descending from the clouds and at the same time a human, so it seems that the phrase has undergone a re-invention under the early church. Perhaps the historical Jesus really did refer to himself as the son of man, and his Jewish audience would have identified the title as meaning that Jesus was a mortal being.

Conclusions

The only way to understand the real Jesus is to examine the world in which he inhabited, only then can we hope to catch a glimpse of him and what his true message was. The Israel of his time was not a happy one, there was a common belief that these were evil times and that soon God would turn the tides of history and bring about a period of justice for the Jews. When Jesus, therefore, appears and preaches about the Kingdom of God, he is doing nothing extraordinary for this time. Several scholars, including G Vermes, P Fredriksen and EP Sanders, have interpreted Jesus as a Jewish holy man with precisely this kind of drastic expectation and his entire mission is focused on the belief that the Kingdom of God would descend shortly. If we can accept that Jesus believed the Kingdom was at hand it can certainly help us understand the apparent urgency of his mission as he darts from community to community urging his followers to reject their wealth, leave their families and turn to God.

Of course, there was an expectation that a man would arrive to usher in this new dawn for Israel. Eventually, perhaps in his own lifetime, Jesus was hailed as this awaited one and his messiahship is preached among the very first Christians, both Jewish and Gentile. It was his followers, the original disciples, his own brother and Paul who continued his message. As his teaching spread outside of the Galilee and took hold around the region and ultimately grew roots in Rome itself, the image of Jesus changed. He was no longer esteemed by Jews but by former pagans and they increasingly interpreted his life according to pagan eyes. Consequently, Jesus was more than a mere messiah - he was God himself in human form. Jesus had acquired divinity, he was the literal Son of God as the Gentile mind would have understood it. As a divinity it was easier to understand how he could have performed various miracles and healings attributed to him. It is to these miracles that we now turn as we try to understand what they meant and whether there is any truth behind them.

CHAPTER FIVE

The Meaning of Miracles

In the year 793 CE the Anglo-Saxon chronicles record a remarkable incident when dragons were spotted in the skies of northern England:

> *"This year came dreadful fore-warnings over the land of the Northumbrians, terrifying the people most woefully: these were immense sheets of light rushing through the air, and whirlwinds, and fiery dragons flying across the firmament."*

These dread inspiring events were seen as omens of things to come. In this case, the appearance of dragons would usher in a famine and the invasion of Danish raiders.

Since the beginning of recorded history, people have always observed strange phenomenon in the sky. Did the ancient Anglo-Saxons see real dragons? Likely not. Yet it is easy to forgive them for harboring such beliefs. The ancients lacked our modern preoccupation with scientific method and were soaked in centuries of lore; the seas were filled with colossal serpents, famine could be bought about because of collective sin and the actions of a bird could determine whether a patient would live or die. These were different times to our own.

What is interesting is how, when explaining extraordinary events, the witness will naturally revert back to their own culture to seek an explanation. The Anglo-Saxon chroniclers perhaps did see something strange on the horizon and interpreted it as dragons because the early British culture was filled with stories of horrific creatures best seen in the epic poem Beowulf. These days alien visitors would be blamed, being as we are so molded by half a century of b-movies.

We must understand that the ancients had their own way of viewing the world which is in stark contrast to our current world view. Where we look up at the sky and see a series of planets, galaxies and star clusters, the ancients would have understood these as perforations in a sphere that was enveloping the ground below. Beyond this sphere was the domain of the angels.

The gospels record several amazing events that if witnessed today would truly be evidence of the supernatural at work. Among his miracles, Jesus was said to be able to heal the sick, he turned water into wine and he was even able to bring the dead back to life. But, saying that Jesus was a miracle worker based on the testimony of the gospels is the same as concluding the ancient Britons were actually plagued by dragons. We cannot logically reject the Anglo-Saxon dragons but at the same time accept the miracles of Jesus. It is better to reject all fantastic stories in the sources as products of ancient cultures.

The best way to understand the miracles of Jesus is to accept that the ancients had a fundamentally different world view to our own, but also understand the inherent symbolism behind them. The Anglo-Saxons witnessed dragons as an omen of impending danger from the heathen invaders. The dragons were symbolic of trouble to come and behind Jesus' miracles also lay a wealth of symbolism.

What Miracles Did Jesus Supposedly Perform?

The gospels are brimming with incidents in which Jesus seems to suspend the very laws of nature, and reading through the Book of Acts we also see that there was a continuation of miraculous healing by the first Christians. All of this suggests that Jesus was known as a miracle worker in his own lifetime.

Jesus' miracles are commonly understood by modern Christians as evidencing that he is God. As a divinity it is easy to understand how he could manipulate the laws of nature, he wrote them, he can bend them. Yet Jesus was a Jew of the first century, a wise man perhaps, a teacher, a prophet, but not an omnipresent God. Of course these miracles, strongly attested as they are in the gospels, must be understood in the context of an ancient, primitive society.

At any rate, these miracles can be neatly divided into four distinct categories: he was able to heal the sick, exorcise demons from the bodies of the possessed, control nature and he could raise the dead.

His ability to heal is described more in the synoptic gospels and less in John. The four gospels contain accounts of Jesus healing dropsy (an old term for swelling of the soft tissues), lameness, paralysis, deafness, a withered arm, fever and a hemorrhage. These healings are mentioned only once. More commonly, Jesus is described as healing blindness (there are three accounts of this type of healing) and leprosy (two accounts).

Regarding exorcisms, there are seven major events of this type of miracle in the synoptic gospels, but none in John. Commonly, some number of evil spirits or demons had possessed the body of an otherwise innocent person and Jesus is called on to assist. Through addressing the demon Jesus is able to command it to leave the body. Once the demon is gone the formerly possessed person then is able to continue their life.

During his travels Jesus is able to manipulate the environment. This cluster of miracles includes his famous ability to turn water into wine, to walk on water, to catch a large amount of fish and feed a multitude of people with a small supply of food. His lesser known nature miracles include his cursing of a fig tree and his finding a coin in a fish's mouth.

Finally, Jesus in the gospels is able to raise the dead; Mark reports that Jesus raised the daughter of Jairus, Luke records the raising of the young man from Nain and John presents to us the raising of Lazarus.

Seen together alongside Jesus' teachings, the miracles serve to show us that his mission did indeed possess authority - that Jesus had a power that ultimately derived from God (and later to evidence that Jesus was that God) and therefore we should heed the content of his teaching. But what are the skeptics to make of these incidents? Are these the mere imaginings of his biased biographers, or is the situation more complicated than that? Of course, we should seek to understand the context into which these events occurred and to do this we shall first examine Jesus' healing ability and the understanding of what caused disease in these times.

What Were The Ancient Causes and Treatments of Diseases?

It is only very recently that we have come to understand such things as infections, bacteria and viruses. Even as late as the nineteenth century there was still a common assumption that cholera was caused by miasma – bad air accompanied by a foul smell. Only with further advances in medicine did we discover the real cause of cholera and then understood suitable measures to prevent it. Long before the scientific method came into practice, the ancients could have no solid understanding of the real cause of disease.

The Romans had inherited a system of medicine that was based largely on their Greek predecessors' work. For centuries medical thought revolved around the actions of the four humors: blood, yellow and black bile and phlegm (representing the four elements of air, fire, earth and water) which when out of balance could cause disease. To treat illness meant trying to get the body into balance again. For example, a prescription of herbs could reduce or increase the incidence of a particular humor as required, or as was popular; opening a vein to drain the body of blood could readdress an excess of this humor. This methodology was first expounded by Hippocrates but survived in western medicine for centuries until the advent of modern medicine. Practitioners of this kind of medicine, because they sought to understand the process going on inside the body, were the forerunners of our modern doctors. The sick could, therefore, choose to visit a physician to illicit a cure, but where this was not viable (this type of treatment was expensive with often exorbitant doctor's fees) patients had other recourses.

Citizens of Rome, during Jesus' time, might have preferred to seek treatment in a sanctuary of Asclepius, the Greek healing god whose cult continued into the Roman era. Typically, the patient would enter the temple, leaving offerings and prayers, and while sleeping in the temple they hoped to be visited by the Asclepius and consequently healed. Asclepius first gained a popular following sometime around 300 BCE but the ancients would continue to visit his numerous shrines long into the Christian era.

But there was another type of lay person in the ancient context who could also provide treatment. We have a set of scrolls called the Magic Papyri dating from the second century BCE all the way until the fifth century CE, which illustrate that magic was commonly practiced in the ancient world to treat sickness. The papyri describe magical recipes that could be made, which included such exotic items as bats eyes to ward off negative influences.

Invocations to powerful deities were also made in the hope that the power of this being would assist in curing the patient. Interestingly, within the Papyri the name of the Jewish God, Yahweh, is recognized as one such powerful entity and his name was likely invoked in the healing process by pagan magicians.

In many ways, these different methods of treating disease were all interlinked. It was not unusual for a physician to call upon a deity for assistance, and they often used natural ingredients in the same way that magicians might use them. Yet it is clear that that cures could be elicited through both medicinal and miraculous methods and the same seems to be true of Israel in this period.

During the time of Jesus, some of the above mentioned methods of treatment were used by the Jews, for example the community of Essenes at Qumran are known to have been familiar with the Greco-Roman methodologies of medicine as evidenced by fragments of a scroll which appears to be a medicinal report for one patient which adheres to standard Hellenistic medicinal method. Yet at this most eastern fringe of the Roman Empire, the Jewish people had a slightly different view as to the cause and treatment of various ailments. In this period, the uniquely Jewish concept of sin was also regarded as a factor that could cause illness. If a Jew were to contravene a moral law of God he would be considered a sinner and a consequence of sin was sickness. This attitude is reflected in the gospels, in John, for example, Jesus tells a man who he has just healed to *"stop sinning or something worse will happen to you."*[75]

Of course, God was present in all occasions and knew when one was being good or bad, and thus could

---

[75] John 5:14

proscribe a punishment. The patient would have to offer suitable atonement in the form of sacrifice and purification in order to alleviate the symptoms. In a previous chapter we saw how Jesus told a leper to report to the Temple priests to fulfill the required purification ritual, this was a cleansing of sin and thus a way to remove illness.

Evidence also exists from the Qumran community that sins could be pardoned by certain members of society. *"I was afflicted with an evil ulcer for seven years...and a gazer pardoned my sins,"* is a section of the Prayer of Nabondius' found in fragments in the Qumran cave 4. A gazer is postulated by G Vermes to be some type of soothsayer. It was possible for this kind of person to actually forgive sins and thereby reduce the associated symptoms.

At Jericho, a blind man known as the Son of Timaues approached and called to Jesus, he is healed and Jesus says *"your faith has healed you."*[76] This is an incident that is remarkably similar to the sick man's petition to the gazer mentioned above. Here, Jesus is the one who is able to forgive sins through the patient's faith in God. Having faith and living a sinless life is a recipe for health in this view and Jesus as one close with God could also inspire faith in those around him and remove their illnesses.

We have to remind ourselves that these were different times and so when a miraculous healing is reported in the gospels, or indeed in any ancient text, we should therefore take particular care to understand that the ancients had no solid scientific knowledge of the cause and effects of disease.

---

[76] Mark 10:52

Could Jesus Miraculously Heal People?

The gospels say that Jesus could heal through a variety of methods, quite often involving physical touch. In one case, a very weak person is struggling to get the attention of Jesus and manages to touch the hem of his cloak (his tassels) and Jesus can sense that some power is drained from him (which implies that Jesus had a limited reserve of power).[77] In other cases, Jesus is said to be able to heal from a distance, without touching or even seeing the sick person.

If one had only the bible to read then Jesus' ability to heal would seem extraordinary but as it is Jesus is not alone among the ancients in being able to perform miracle healings. A blind man approached the Roman Emperor Titus Flavius Vespasian and asked the ruler to heal his blindness, *"and he besought the emperor to deign to moisten his cheeks and eyes with his spittle,"* (in ancient times spit was held to have strong healing properties). After some debate as to whether or not it was a good idea to attempt such a cure, for he feared that failure would lead to ridicule, Vespasian relents and does as asked and *"the day shone again for the blind man."* To further add weight to this incident the writer, Tacitus, mentions that eyewitnesses were also present.[78]

Taken at face value this intriguing incident would seem miraculous. However, like any ancient text one has to read between the lines. In this case, there has been a change in the Roman ruling elite; no longer is the Julio-Claudian family in power, now it is the turn of the Flavians. Any change of dynasty will naturally elicit some level of dissent among supporters of the former regime and Tacitus wants to show that the people should trust in their new ruler. Tacitus is the first to admit that

---

[77] see Luke 8:46
[78] Tacitus, The Histories 4.81

under the patronage of Vespasian his own position in life had greatly increased. Clearly, Tacitus is in favor of his benefactor and his writing is a piece of propaganda designed to show that his master was a great ruler – so great that he could even perform miraculous healings!

Mark records an incident at a village called Bethsaida. Some people bring a blind man to Jesus and beg him to heal the unfortunate man. Jesus took him outside of the village and *"when he had spit on the man's eyes and put his hands on him,"* Jesus asked, *"do you see anything?"* Of course, he could.[79] The thing that is striking in this story is Jesus' use of spit in the healing of the man, something that never appears in any paintings or movies of Jesus, but something that very likely occurred. This reflects the ancient belief in the power of spittle to heal, and it is interesting to see it used by both Jesus and Vespasian, but does Mark, like Tacitus also include any elements of propaganda? And if so, what is he actually trying to relate to us?

Just as we can understand Tacitus through a brief glimpse of the broader picture, so too can we understand the gospels. The gospel writers want us to believe their point of view, want us to believe in the figure of Jesus, and so his ability to heal is used as evidence so that we may hear and believe his broader teachings. Jesus taught and he healed, therefore he has power and we should listen to him. This seems to be the underlying message behind Jesus' miracle healings.

If we are looking for a more symbolic meaning of his miracles we should remember that Jesus also taught that the Kingdom of God was close. In the new epoch of heavenly justice there was to be no disease. Jesus' healings are a symbolic precursor to a time when

---

[79] Mark 8:22-26

disease would no longer cause suffering. Jesus is offering us a glimpse into the Kingdom of God, which was a central and important aspect of his teachings as expressed in the gospels.

The true meaning of his healings, as the evangelists have it, is summed up by an incident that is common to Matthew and Luke and therefore a Q document source. John the Baptist has heard rumors of Jesus' work and sends some of his own followers to ask Jesus whether he is the one they have been waiting for. *"At that very time Jesus cured many who had diseases, sicknesses and evil spirits, and gave sight to many who were blind. So he replied to the messengers, 'Go back and report to John what you have seen and heard: The blind receive sight, the lame walk, those who have leprosy are cured, the deaf hear, the dead are raised, and the good news is preached to the poor.'"*[80] Jesus' healings are understood here as evidencing the approaching Kingdom of God and serve to bolster Jesus' messianic claim.

In one Jewish text known as the Book of Enoch, which was possibly written and edited between 300-100 BCE but wasn't contained in either the Jewish or Christian canon, healing is explicitly linked with the divine renewal of Israel. This demonstrates that Jesus' own healings were not unprecedented within the Judaism of his time and took place in a broader context of an expectation of Israel's redemption. Thus, when Jesus tells John that the sick are healed he means that the Kingdom is coming.

The first readers of the gospels, both Jewish and Gentile, would have understood Jesus to be a powerful healer and would have therefore paid more attention to his central message. His healings were signs that his words

---

[80] Luke 7:21-22

were true and this is precisely why the gospels place a strong emphasis on them. Then again, Tacitus' readers would have understood the Emperor Vespasian's healing as indicative of his greatness and that was simple propaganda.

Of course, our modern knowledge of science prevents us from believing in miraculous healing, we think of autosuggestion or the placebo effect as a possible explanation for faith healing, but then the ancients lacked our modern way of seeing things. To the ancients miraculous healings were both possible and plausible. There was no reason for them to doubt that miracles, although unlikely and rare incidents, were possible. In that respect, Jesus had demonstrated miraculous healing, and his well attested ability to perform them helps us moderns to understand how his teaching spread so rapidly beyond the confines of Judaism.

Could Jesus Exorcise Demons?

The second category of miracles demonstrated by Jesus, according to the gospels, is closely related to those of his healing actions because demons were also understood to be a cause of sickness within both the Jewish and the Gentile context. Since Jesus is described as being able to expel these creatures from the bodies of their victims he is healing them of their illness. The gospels give us seven well developed examples of Jesus expelling demons and consequently curing an affliction.

That the belief in demons was common in the time of Jesus can be in no doubt, Josephus for example records a property of a certain root in the treatment of one possessed by a demon and says that *"it is only valuable on account of one virtue it hath, that if it be only brought to sick persons, it quickly drives away those called demons, which are no other than the spirits of the wicked, that enter into men that are alive and kill them, unless they can obtain some help against them."*[81] He also describes how one Eleazar expels a demon from a man by placing a ring with some suitable roots under his nose and calling on the name of Solomon and uttering some incantations so that the demon promptly leaves the body.

If the ancients had very little understanding of the working of pathogens then they knew practically nothing of mental illness. Insanity was commonly believed to be a result of demonic possession. In the gospels we can see various characters exhibiting signs of mental afflictions as this example demonstrates:

"When Jesus got out of the boat, a man with an evil spirit came from the tombs to meet him. This man lived in the tombs, and no one could bind him any more, not even with a chain. For he had often been chained hand and foot, but he tore the chains apart and broke the irons on his feet. No one was strong enough to subdue him. Night and day among the tombs and in the hills he would cry out and cut himself with stones."[82] If this were a modern description there is little doubt that this poor fellow would be suffering from some type of mental affliction – indeed some have gone on to propose a diagnosis of Schizophrenia or even Epilepsy.

Belief in demons was certainly widespread and it is not surprising that there were many who were regarded as having the power to exorcise them. This is evidenced in the gospels when one of the disciples reports to Jesus, *"we saw a man driving out demons in your name and we told him to stop, because he was not one of us."*[83] Perhaps this example is a reflection on the fact that many pagan magicians quickly came to regard Christians as possessing strong magic and considered the name of Jesus as an effective charm against illness in a similar

---

[81] Jewish War 6.3.11
[82] Mark 5:1-10
[83] Mark 9:38

way in which the name of Yahweh was used in the Magical Papyri.

Some scholars have even interpreted Jesus as a magician, but in this era magic was something thoroughly distasteful. Mark preserves some disgust at Jesus' exorcisms when Jesus is accused of driving out demons because he himself is possessed. Some teachers of the law say *"He is possessed by Beelzebub! By the prince of demons he is driving out demons."*[84] It is interesting that these teachers did not doubt Jesus' powers but instead attributed them to the ancient Philistine deity of biblical notoriety.

Mark's Jesus is very reticent about his true identity. After healing someone Jesus often urges his patient to tell no one of what has transpired. Interestingly, Mark uses the demons as a plot device to reveal Jesus' true identity. The demon exorcised at the synagogue in Capernaum says *"What do you want with us, Jesus of Nazareth? Have you come to destroy us? I know who you are – the Holy One of God!"*[85] Just as Jesus' healings revealed the truth of the coming Kingdom, so too his exorcisms were pointing ahead to this event. The purpose of Jesus' exorcisms is neatly summed up in Luke *"But if I drive out demons by the finger of God, then the Kingdom of God has come to you."*[86] Everything contained within the gospels is placed there to support the belief of the evangelists, in this case the Kingdom of God would contain no demons. Jesus' exorcisms thus give added substance to his teachings about the Kingdom.

There are examples of demonic possession and exorcism in both the Jewish and Gentile contexts. It is not unreasonable, therefore, to suggest that the historical Jesus was also an exorcist. Though not as

---

[84] Mark 3:22
[85] Mark 1:24
[86] Luke 11:20

well attested in the gospels as Jesus' healing, because John makes no mention of them, exorcisms would continue to be a feature of Christianity in its formative years. Paul claimed to be able drive away demons by touch and indeed exorcisms by the Catholic Church continue even today.

Of course, today we strive to understand something of the causes of mental illness but to the ancients madness was the result of demonic possession so when we read of Jesus expelling demons we are reminded that he was active in a bygone era where such events were hardly extraordinary. His exorcisms cannot therefore be regarded as truly miraculous merely the result of pre-scientific understanding struggling to understand phenomenon that were beyond their intellectual grasp.

What Does Jesus' Control Over Nature Symbolize?

Jesus' healings and his exorcisms probably derive from a historical reality, that is in his own lifetime Jesus was a purveyor of the miraculous which as we have seen is not in itself an extraordinary proposition according to the standards of the day. The gospel writers are clear that his wonder workings were symbolic of a deeper meaning, they were signs that Jesus spoke with authority and that his words should be headed – this was the messiah and the Kingdom of God was at hand.

Many so-called miraculous events in antiquity are symbolic of a greater, deeper meaning. Thus dragons and comets are omens and portents of bad things to come, and for Vespasian his healings were meant to show that he possessed imperial authority. What then lies behind Jesus' ability to control nature? What are these miracles showing us?

Naturally, Christians and secular historians will have their own interpretations of Jesus' nature miracles but since we are endeavoring to understand the historical Jesus we should proceed with a view to discovering plausible symbolic meanings lying behind them. When we remember that every author, including the gospel writers, is subject to the bias of their own times and influenced by their desire to get their point across these nature miracles can be seen in a new light. Provided here are three nature miracles with common historical interpretations of their meaning.

CALMING THE STORM

Jesus calming a storm is an interesting story given in each of the synoptic gospels. Jesus is with his disciples on a boat in the Sea of Galilee, as it happens the leader of this group is fast asleep on a cushion when a storm suddenly rises. The waves crash into the boat and the disciples fear that they will be drowned so they wake up Jesus hoping for some reassurance. Perhaps giddy from being awoken by his followers he calms the storm before rebuking them for their lack of faith. What is the symbolic meaning behind this intriguing story?

Most likely, the event can be seen as a euphemism for the environment in which the gospels are being compiled; we have seen how the Kingdom of God was supposed to come imminently and that Christians believed that Jesus would be returning within their own lifetimes. While they were waiting, however, they were already suffering the consequences of their belief. Nero was blaming Christians for starting the Great Fire of Rome and using them as human candles to illuminate his palace gardens, and there may have been other persecutions because of the former pagan's refusal to offer sacrifices to the traditional gods. They were suffering terribly for their beliefs and many must have wondered where Jesus was? And where was the Kingdom of God that he promised?

Symbolically speaking, these distraught believers were like the disciples in the boat. They were being rocked by a terrible storm and Jesus seemed to be sleeping. The moral of the story is to have faith in Jesus; he will come soon and will quiet the storm. The followers are reminded to keep their faith and surely things would ultimately be better. Indeed faith seems to be an important ingredient to the other miracles. When Jesus walks on water Peter tries to follow but he becomes afraid when he saw the wind and he panics as he begins to sink. Jesus reaches out his hand to save Peter, *"'You of little faith,' he said, 'why did you doubt?'"*[87]

WATER INTO WINE

John's gospel has Jesus attending a wedding when his mother comes to him and warns that the guests will be without wine. Jesus orders the servants to fill the pots with water and then serve it to the master of the banquet. When it is served it is discovered that the water has become wine.

They key to understanding this story is this line, *"Nearby stood six stone water jars, the kind used by the Jews for ceremonial washing."*[88] The jars then had a connection with ritual purification whereby water is used to wash the hands before eating. Now instead of water, there is wine. This is best understood as symbolic that the old practices of Judaism (such as ritual purification) are no longer valid to John's Christian community. Jesus has come, in John's view, and created something all together new. The rest of John's gospel is very much Hellenistic in nature and his highly developed divine Christ represents a distinct step away from the Jewish

---

[87] Matthew 14:22-33
[88] John 2:6

origins of Christianity. This story is a symbolic representation of John's belief.

This story is missing from the synoptic gospels, and is unique only to John. However, the synoptics do present a parable of new wine into old wineskins, which may share common origins with John's more developed story. When wine was being fermented it was placed into new wineskins. During the fermentation process gases would be released causing the skins to expand and then harden. Thus to put new wine into old wineskins would risk rupturing the skin. This parable, recorded in each of the synoptics, has been interpreted by Christians to mean that Jesus was starting a new religion, one that was not compatible with the old skins of Judaism's past. But the parable, and indeed John's story, may also hint at certain biblical prophecies that in the age of the messiah there would be an abundance of wine.

The actual event of Jesus turning water into wine probably did not happen or was based on the prophecy and developed into a story by John. What is obvious is the symbolism of John's opinion that Jewish law, represented by the pots, is redundant and a new movement had begun.

FEEDING THE FIVE THOUSAND

The story of Jesus' miraculous feeding of the five thousand enjoys multiple attestations, being present in all four of the gospels, which suggests at its core there is a grain of historical truth behind the event. Certainly we know that Jesus attracted large crowds and it is possible that this story originates in an actual incident, although of course by the time it was recorded in the gospels it would have already suffered from exaggeration.

In the story, a large assembly of people has gathered to hear Jesus speak but there is not enough food to go around. To resolve this, Jesus prays over the few pieces of food that is available, some bread and a couple of fish, and then there is suddenly food enough for everyone. What symbolism is recorded in this story?

In the Book of Exodus, Moses is leading the Israelites into the desert but they are complaining about all of the food that they had left behind in Egypt. To resolve this, Moses prays to God who sends down loaves of bread from the sky. Jesus' own provision of bread is symbolic of his predecessor's deeds and just as Moses revolutionized Judaism, Jesus too was bringing about an important change.

The prophet Elisha described in the Book of Kings is also able to provide enough food for a smaller crowd. He manages to feed one hundred men with just twenty loaves of bread.[89] Jesus it seems can feed more with less. Thus, the gospels are trying to convince us that Jesus is not merely another prophet; he is the ultimate and most powerful.

Could Jesus Raise The Dead?

There are exactly three occasions when Jesus is said to have bought back a person from the dead. Mark contains the story of the daughter of Jairus, a young girl who had died. Jesus arrives and commands *'Talitha Koum'* which means 'little girl rise,' and she does. Luke has the story of the son of the widow of Nain in which Jesus comes across a funeral procession and a widowed mother is burying her only son. Jesus commands *"young man, I say to you, arise!"* and the corpse does as commanded. Finally, John contains the story of Lazarus who has already spent four days dead in his tomb. Jesus tells the family to roll open the stone and cries out *"Lazarus, come forth!"* and to the awe of those assembled Lazarus emerges.

---

[89] See 2 Kings 4:42-44

It is possible that Jesus' bringing the dead back to life is a tradition that contains a thimble of historic truth. This, of course, does not mean that historians accept that bodily resurrection is in any way possible, merely this is what his early followers, based on their belief in the possibility, thought had happened, which will be examined later.

Once again, we have to try to understand the mindset of the people among whom these miraculous stories first appealed and circulated. Within the gospels there are some interesting clues that we can examine to determine the extent to which belief in resurrection was possible in this era. John the Baptist was killed by Herod, but the nefarious king, upon hearing the words and deeds of Jesus is disconcerted. Mark tells us that, *"Some were saying, 'John the Baptist has been raised from the dead, and that is why miraculous powers are at work in him [Jesus].'"*[90]

The fact that these people speculate whether the Baptist has come back from the dead highlights the presupposition that it is possible in their worldview for this type of miracle to occur. We also know that among Jews of this time there was a debate over whether the dead could indeed be resurrected. The Pharisees expected the dead to rise again and their natural enemies the Sadducees supposed resurrection was impossible. Some in this period were, therefore, inclined to believe that resurrection was a possibility and Jesus' miracles would fit into this intellectual frame of mind. They were consequently more likely to believe the miraculous tales that they had heard about Jesus raising the dead.

We have to remember that the prime purpose of Jesus' mission in Mark and the synoptic gospels is to announce the coming Kingdom of God. The messiah

---

[90] Mark 6:14

has arrived and a new dawn is going to be ushered onto the world, a dawn that will see the defeat of injustice, no more disease, no more demons and no more death. Jesus' actions then must be framed within this scene and his own miraculous ability to raise the dead can, therefore, be seen as a symbolic precursor to this time when death itself will cease to exist.

Jesus was not alone among the Jewish prophets in having the ability to raise the dead. A story contained in the First Book of Kings bears striking resemblance to the tales told about Jesus. In this case, Elijah meets a mother and son but when the son dies Elijah calls to God to allow his life to return. The son is resurrected and the mother proclaims that Elijah is a man of God.[91]

There are numerous and remarkable parallels between Elijah's miracle and Luke's story of the resurrection of the young man at Nain:

"As he approached the town gate, a dead person was being carried out – the only son of his mother, and she was a widow."[92]

Jesus encounters, just as Elijah did, a funeral procession with a widow who is burying her son. This is not merely a coincidence because the connection between the two incidents is purposeful. Luke's story is a theological invention designed to show the similarities between Jesus and the great prophet Elijah.

Elijah does make an actual appearance in the synoptic gospels during the curious incident known as the transfiguration of Jesus. Here, Jesus is climbing a mountain when he starts to radiate a light and the accompanying disciples see him in conversation with both Moses and Elijah. This serves to show us that the

---

[91] See 1 kings 17:7-24
[92] Luke 7:12

gospel writers believed Jesus to be a powerful man, not merely in line with the traditional Jewish prophets but superseding them because the voice of God proclaims Jesus his 'son' and then the two other prophets disappear leaving Jesus and his stunned disciples alone.

No one will ever know for sure how the stories of the dead coming back to life originated. Perhaps, there was a grain of truth that became later exaggerated when the stories began circulating orally. Possibly, they are an invention by the evangelists. What is clear, however, is that some Jews believed that the raising of dead was a possibility, and some evidently believed that all dead would rise in the Kingdom of God. These peoples were receptive to resurrection stories and were more likely to believe the extraordinary tales that were being uttered about the man from Nazareth. In the end, however, it would have been more miraculous if Jesus was said to have raised the dead in a religious environment in which there was no precedent for such a thing.

How Unique Are Jesus' Miraculous Abilities?

Jesus was not alone among the ancients in supposedly possessing miraculous abilities. Both within the biblical tradition and without there are numerous examples of men who were regarded as possessing special powers. Presented here are the examples of three other historical miracle workers whose lives are roughly contemporary with Jesus'. One of them is a Gentile and the other two are Jews, but their lives show a remarkable similarity with Jesus'. A glimpse into their lives can help us to understand several things, namely how the ancients were inclined to believe in miracle workers, and then through a comparison of the type of miracles performed we can better understand that Jesus was not at all extraordinary, indeed, from this perspective Jesus seems to fit into an archetype of first century miracle workers.

APOLLONIUS OF TYANA

Although the exact dates of the life of Apollonius are hazy, he nevertheless was active before the Christian era and his life was roughly contemporary with Jesus'. From analyzing the content Philostratus' Life of Apollonius of Tyana (the main biography of Apollonius) written in the second century and the mention of the Roman Emperors Nero and Vespasian, Apollonius' life can be dated to approximately 15–98 CE.

Apollonius, like Jesus, was a teacher and miracle worker who travelled extensively and his biography in places corresponds intriguingly with that of Jesus'. The first similarities are seen with his birth. Apollonius' mother while pregnant with Apollonius sees an apparition of a Greek god in the guise of an Egyptian demon. Unafraid, the expectant mother asks the being what her future son will be like, to which the deity says Apollonius will be like himself, Proteus. Proteus was a Greek divinity associated with the sea, great wisdom and the ability to foresee the future. As we saw earlier the ancients were of the habit of giving their heroes extraordinary and miraculous births, and in this case Philostratus is trying to explain his subject's own wisdom and foresight by relating them to the divine.

Apollonius is educated and embraces the school of philosophy expounded by Pythagoras but afterwards he travels the world. During his adventures he meets various kings and magi before venturing to the mysterious lands of India where he debates among the learned men present there. In India, Apollonius' miraculous abilities are made known. He is approached by a women whose son is possessed by a demon that *"will not allow him to retain his reason, nor will he permit him to go to school, or to learn archery, nor even to remain at home, but drives him out into desert places. And the boy does not even retain his own voice, but speaks in a deep hollow tone, as men do; and he looks at you with other eyes rather than with his own."* Apollonius writes a letter to the bad spirit which contains some alarming threats and the demon leaves the body of the boy without causing harm.

Another incident has a man being bitten by a mad dog. The victim then starts barking and running around on all fours. Apollonius calls for the dog to be captured but no one knows where it is because the attack occurred outside of the city walls, but thanks to his gift of foresight Apollonius tells them exactly where to find the animal. It is bought back and the philosopher is able to tame it by stroking it. He proclaims that the soul of Telephus of Mysia, a Greek legendary hero, has entered the man. Telephus had been wounded by another hero of old, Achilles, but Achilles had also healed his victim. So with this bizarre logic the dog begins to lick the wound that it has inflicted on the man who promptly recovers. The dog is now free from its own madness and is last spotted wagging its tail with its ears pinned back from across a river.

Besides healing through exorcism, the sage was a social and religious reformer who strove to infuse the pagans with a more moral outlook to life. When the priests of a pagan temple ask him why he does not offer a blood sacrifice like all others, Apollonius counters by questioning why the priest must sacrifice in this way. Apollonius, with his wisdom gained from the Indian mystics is in a position to look back at his own culture and find criticism with it, which reminds us of Jesus' commentary on his Jewish countrymen.

Like Jesus, Apollonius is portrayed as having life after death. In his case, he continued to preach that the soul was immortal even from beyond the grave. A youth who had been praying to Apollonius for nine months hoping to learn the truth of the soul finally meets him in a dream. *"Do you not see,"* the youth says later to his friends, *"Apollonius the sage, how that he is present with us and is listening to our discussion, and is reciting wondrous verses about the soul?"*

Philostratus' account of Apollonius was written a century after the events that it depicts and had already accrued legendary features. Many of the incidents described are likely to be pure fiction while others are exaggerations of historical events. Yet this biography wasn't written to mislead, its author believed that his subject was indeed a powerful man and wrote to convince his audience of this too. He wanted us to believe that Apollonius possessed divine powers and had a moral message. In this respect the similarities with the gospels are numerous.

HONI THE CIRCLE DRAWER

Since the times of Elijah and Elisha it was commonly assumed that those holy men who shared a close relationship with God could perform what today we would call miracles. An example of a later member of the Jewish holy man tradition is that of Honi who is known to us through several ancient texts, including that of Josephus. Like Jesus, Honi was active in the first century. One year, the people were expecting rains but none came so they approached Honi for a solution. Honi drew a circle in the sands and stood within in it and then he called out to God *"Lord of the world, thy children have turned to me because I am as a son of the house before thee. I swear by thy name that I will not move hence until thou be merciful towards thy children."*[93] It begins to drizzle, but this was not enough. He chastises God and the rain increases. But now there is too much. Once again Honi complains until finally there is a sufficient amount of rain.

---

[93] Mishnah Ta'anit

Honi comes across as rather a rude character, especially when his words are compared to the more humble approach to God that Jesus shows. The head of the Sanhedrin in Jerusalem, said to Honi, *"I should excommunicate you for your audacity, but how can I, since you're Honi! God coddles you as a father does his young child. The child says: 'Hold me, Daddy, and bathe me, and give me poppy seeds and peaches and pomegranates,' and his father gives him whatever he wants."*[94]

Honi was almost excommunicated until it was realized that he enjoyed a special kind of relationship with God. Indeed, within the quote above we can see that Honi is described as being a 'son of god's house', which is comparable with the term 'son of god' that was employed by Jesus and indicative of a closeness with God. Honi, within the Jewish tradition is able to manipulate the weather because of this special relationship. Here we see numerous parallels between Jesus and the life of Honi. Both of these men were said to have power over the weather and both were described in terms relating to 'sons of god' or 'sons of god's household.' This allows us to adequately identify Jesus the Jew comfortably sitting within first century Jewish traditions. Jesus is hardly an extraordinary character.

HANINA BEN DOSA

Another first century wonder worker, Hanina Ben Dosa stands firmly within the same miraculous tradition as Honi and Jesus. As in the case with Honi, it is not the man per se who possesses power but instead a closeness with God which allows miracles to be produced.

Hanina, like the other Jewish wonder workers, lives a very humble lifestyle without great riches. Yet this doesn't seem to matter to Hanina (although his wife

---

[94] Mishnah Ta'anit 23a

could do with more) as he is content merely to pray a lot. A story is related of Johanan ben Zakkai (who is Honi's teacher) who calls upon Honi to heal his sick son. Honi complies and the boy is cured. Johanan's wife however, wonders whether this means the student is more powerful than his master. Johanan replies to her, saying *"There is this difference between us: he is like the body-servant of a king, having at all times free access to the august presence [ie the divine presence of God], without even having to await permission to reach his ears; while I, like a lord before a king, must await an opportune moment."*[95] Thanks to his humbleness Hanina enjoys privileged access to God.

Hanina also seems to have excerpted some influence on the weather. In one incident he is annoyed when he is caught in a shower and prays to God who relinquishes the rain. When at last Hanina is at home he prays again and the rain pours down once again. The parallels between Honi the circle drawer are quite clear in this story, both could pray and bring about rain. Both were healers.

From these examples we can see quite evidently that Jesus was not alone among the Jewish holy men in possessing the miraculous power to heal and control the weather. Jesus stands firmly within a very Jewish tradition of these wonder workers. Jesus was a man of his time and his own miracles make sense when we see them in the bigger picture of ancient semi-legendary persons. If these miracles are relatively common among the ancients what does that mean to Jesus' status as a god?

Surely it is diminished.

---

[95] Mishnah Berakhot 34b

Conclusions

Jesus was hardly unique in the ancient world for his ability to perform miracles, as we saw there are numerous examples of wonder workers, many of whom also lived in the first century. These examples demonstrate in the ability of the ancient mind to interpret great men as having powers of divine origin. Today, a spontaneous healing might be explained away as a product of the Placebo effect. To the ancients this was nothing less than the intervention of a higher power.

These wonder workers didn't merely have power for power's sake because there is usually an accompanying message: for Jesus his miracles evidenced the imminence of the Kingdom of God, for Vespasian his healing ability proved his suitability to be Emperor, for Apollonius his teachings on the immortality of the soul were valid, for Honi and Hanina a closeness to God could produce extraordinary feats.

With regards to Jesus, we should understand his miracles not as historical feats of divine power but instead as symbolic to the message he preached. Miracles were used to show that his teaching was authoritative. Moreover, Jesus' miracles were a taste of things to come, a peek into what it would be like when the Kingdom of God finally came.

The Jews would have seen Jesus in the same way in which they understood Honi and Hanina. In other words Jesus could only execute miracles because he was close to God – indeed he is often described as being a 'son of God.' Being close to God meant that the heavenly father was more likely to intervene when his prophet prayed. The power was from God and not from the prophet, but later Christians would claim that Jesus' power derived from his own divinity.

At any rate, Jesus is recognizably Jewish and stands within a tradition of charismatic wonder workers, healers and moral teachers. The pagan Greco-Roman culture also had its own miracle workers and consequently would have been receptive to the idea that Jesus could heal the sick and expel demons from the possessed.

These days we are much less likely to believe in miracles. We quite rightly enjoy asking for proof and we are skeptical about the laws of physics being suspended. To the ancients however, miracles were intellectually possible. There is no reason to doubt that Jews and later the Gentiles would have interpreted Jesus' abilities as actual historical events.

CHAPTER SIX

His Execution and Resurrection

In November 2001, a Nigerian pastor by the name of Daniel Ekechukwu was driving along a road in his home country when the brakes of his car suddenly and dramatically failed. The vehicle smashed headlong into a concrete pillar and for Daniel the situation looked grim. The impact had smashed his internal organs against the ribs and consequently he was suffering internal bleeding and was vomiting blood. He was rushed to hospital and given emergency treatment but Daniel was already preparing for the possibility of an early death. Despite being at death's door, Daniel asks to be transferred to another hospital some eighty kilometers away. During the journey, Daniel dies.

At Umezurike Hospital, the corpse is examined and the doctor confirms to Daniel's wife that her husband is indeed dead. For some reason that is not fully explained, Daniel's body is then taken to various other hospitals in the area until at last he is issued with a death certificate confirming that Daniel had died on Friday 30th November 2001. On the morning of the following Saturday, Daniel's body is kept in a mortuary and embalming chemicals were passed through his body to preserve it.

On the 2nd of December, the body is taken to the Grace of God Mission, a church not far away, and the corpse is placed in the basement. Some people, friends and family of Daniel, have already gathered and were praying. Meanwhile, in the church above, a German evangelist named Reinhard Bonnke was preaching to a congregation of worshipers. As he calls out his impassioned prayers something extraordinary begins to happen. Daniel's body begins to twitch! If this wasn't surprising enough it quickly becomes apparent that Daniel has actually come back to life.

Within no time at all, Daniel is walking and talking and makes a full recovery, which allows him to describe his extraordinary journey through heaven and hell. To many of his eager listeners Daniel's case is nothing short of a miracle. Even the more skeptical among them might have been swayed by the 'evidence' of witnesses and medical reports that proved that Daniel had indeed died.

But was it a miracle? Or was it something else, a hoax perhaps?

Many questions from this case have not been adequately answered. Why for example did Daniel request a hospital transfer when he was dying? Why was his body presented to several hospitals before a death certificate was issued? Subsequent investigations by the renowned Nigerian skeptic Leo Igwe, who personally interviewed some of the witnesses, found numerous inconsistencies in the story. Most notable among these was Daniel's brother who told Mr. Igwe that no embalming chemicals were flooded through the body (the toxic chemicals would have certainly killed whatever life was left in the body).

The preacher Bonnke, then, began to use the 'evidence' of Daniel's amazing resurrection to promote his missionary activities worldwide, even taking Daniel abroad with him. Bonnke, who claims to have converted several million people during his ministry, would certainly be able to convert many more using the miraculous story of Daniel. To the skeptically minded this all seems like an elaborate hoax designed to attract converts to Bonnke's mission. But despite the dubious nature of the miracle many really do believe that Daniel came back to life. Why is this?

Igwe notes the religious conditions prevalent within Nigeria and the peoples' overzealous belief in miracles. Some have even claimed to have healed themselves of HIV through prayers and are so convinced of their new found health that they have had their medical records changed (which suggests that it is not that difficult to get a death certificate). Unfortunately, like most faith healings the world over no one seems to have been back to the doctor to confirm this diagnosis. This is because visiting a doctor for a second diagnosis would demonstrate that you didn't have enough faith in the first place and therefore the healer could not be held accountable if you were found to be still sick.

Stories like Daniel's can only flourish in societies where there is a strong background belief in the possibility of miracles. The Nigerian Christians evidently match this criterion and many among them have taken up the Daniel saga as evidence of the power of God. Certainly, if there were no Christians in Nigeria, and no belief in the possibility of resurrection, then Daniel's story could not be possible.

Our cultural background does indeed influence what we see. Thanks to centuries of Christian influence there is a strong belief that the dead can, and will one day be reanimated. Christians are more likely to believe Daniel rose from the dead because their religious background has colored the way they understand the world.

Turning the clock back to Jesus' time it is possible to see that some sects within Judaism had a strong belief that the dead could be raised. The Pharisees adhered to this view while the Sadducees rejected it. Jesus supported the

Pharisees on this point and he preached that the dead would rise when the Kingdom of God arrived. We can, therefore, say that many of his followers would have been pre-disposed to the possibility of bodily resurrection and consequently were more likely to imagine that Jesus himself had come back from the dead.

How Did Jesus Die?

Jesus lived, ironically, to die. At least this is how the gospels have it. The events leading to his arrest, trial and execution and his strange appearances after death are above all else the most powerful images of the Christian story. Despite two millennia of internal squabbling over trifling matters of theology almost every Christian denomination today adheres to the doctrine that Jesus was raised from the dead after his crucifixion. To understand Jesus you must understand his death.

Despite their obvious bias, we must turn to the gospels in order to discover more details of Jesus' death because they are our only sources on the subject. We must filter through all of the later theology and symbolism and use the gospels to build a picture of his last days. Although the four gospels disagree on several notable points, particularly concerning the timing of events and who Jesus was questioned by at his trial, they all do agree that Jesus was arrested, trialed, sentenced, crucified and resurrected.

Jesus' downfall begins during a time of celebration. When he enters Jerusalem on one or two donkeys he is entering during the festival of the Passover, a time when Jews remember how they were freed from Egyptian slavery by the will of God. The scene would have been extremely chaotic since families would come, many thousands of them, from all around the region to offer the correct sacrifice at the temple. They had been commanded by God to bring a young lamb or a wild goat and present it to a priest at the Temple so that it may be killed according to the necessary ritual. Once the animal was dispatched, the family would take the meat away and prepare it carefully; the head, feet and organs had to be removed and then the meat had to be roasted. Care was taken not to contravene any of the laws specified in the Book of Exodus for the preparation, and as such, no bones were to be broken and the meat had to be consumed before the next morning.

The scene would have been terrific, with thousands of priests, pilgrims and animals and all associated spectacles of sound and smell, but the mass of Jews descending on the city naturally unnerved the Roman overseers. Big crowds meant trouble. So, every year Pilate would order the garrison of troops from Caesarea to Jerusalem to provide extra security. There were some Jews among the multitude who hated the Romans and their pagan ways while some of the more extreme among them had been known to riot during these festivals. Josephus actually remarks that *"It is on these festive occasions that sedition is most apt to break out."*[96] During Passover, the Romans therefore would have been extremely vigilant.

Jesus would be among those regarded as a troublemaker. In the synoptic gospels, Jesus is portrayed as angrily chasing away the moneychangers from the grounds of the Temple and chastising them for turning a holy place into a den of thieves (John has the same incident as the synoptic version but at the beginning of his gospel). What the historical Jesus actually said can never be known, the pilgrims would

---

[96] Jewish War 1.4.3

have needed to change their Roman coin to the Jewish currency for use within the temple because the law specified only the traditional shekel could be used in the Temple, but the gospel writers want us to believe that he is cleansing the Temple. Either way, any kind of disturbance at this time would have irked the Roman authorities and perhaps this was why Jesus was arrested. Certainly, historically speaking this is a possibility, yet after the incident at the Temple the gospels say that Jesus continues to preach in the city. The authorities have not come for him yet but he knows they will very shortly arrest him, so according to the gospels he now has his last supper. With the twelve disciples, Jesus offers bread and wine as a symbol of his own body and blood.

The next day, Jesus is in the garden of Gethsemane- a valley on the eastern side of Jerusalem. He is alone praying when a ruckus occurs. He turns to see his disciple Judas Iscariot followed by several of the Temple guards. Judas identifies his former master by kissing him and thus the authorities now know whom it is they are seeking. Presumably, they could not recognize Jesus without an informer despite the fact that Jesus has been turning tables at the Temple and was accompanied by large numbers of followers. They promptly arrest him, but at least one of his followers resists, draws a sword and strikes a blow at the temple guard which severs his ear. Jesus is lead away and taken to the high priest but the swordsman seems to have escaped justice at this time.

The Sanhedrin, a Jewish council of judges, assembles during the night and Jesus is charged with threatening to destroy the Temple and they conclude that he is blaspheming by claiming to be the messiah (in Mark and Matthew only). Is this picture likely? Since the penalty for blaspheming was death, the Sanhedrin could have ordered the execution themselves. The Book of Acts, in describing the death of Stephan, makes it clear that the Sanhedrin had this authority, as does Josephus' account of the death of James the Just. For reasons that will become apparent later, the gospels say that the Sanhedrin lacked the power to execute anyone so instead they refer Jesus to the Romans.

Pontius Pilate, at first, wants nothing to do with the case. He questions Jesus as to whether he is the king of the Jews. After Jesus relays his teaching Pilate, in John's gospel, is made to declare *"you are a king then!"*[97] And Jesus openly admits that Pilate is correct. John's character of Pilate can find nothing wrong with Jesus and no basis for a charge against him and in a last ditch attempt to save Jesus he offers the Jewish crowd a choice between saving Jesus or another prisoner called Barabbas. Although Jesus has enjoyed popular support among the people they now turn against him and instead begin to shout *"crucify, crucify!"* This contradiction is more apparent in the synoptics, especially after the crowd had so keenly welcomed him into Jerusalem with cheers of 'hosanna.'

Jesus is led away. He is beaten, humiliated and finally crucified. He lingers on the cross for a moment before he dies. The moment of his death is highly dramatic in the accounts. In Matthew Jesus' death is accompanied by earthquakes, the splitting of the curtain in the temple and the bodies of many holy people spontaneously rising from their tombs and going into Jerusalem.

The soldiers want to break Jesus' legs to ensure he is dead (apparently breaking the legs would cause the weight of the body to push down, which effectively

---

[97] John 18:37

suffocates the victim) but they find he is already deceased. A spear is plunged into his side for good measure. The body is taken down with permission from Pilate by a certain man named Joseph of Arimathea, who is unheard of in the gospels prior to this incident. Together, with Nicodemus, they prepare the body for burial, wrapping it up with linen and laying the corpse in a tomb. The story doesn't end there. Later, Mary Magdalene sees that the stone that was sealing the tomb has been moved and the body is gone. She runs back to inform the disciples who practically race back to the tomb to find the burial cloth neatly arranged but the body gone.

Why Do The Soldiers Want Jesus' Underwear?

"When the soldiers crucified Jesus, they took his clothes, dividing them into four shares, one for each of them, with the undergarment remaining."[98]

The gospel of John contains this interesting incident of the Roman soldiers sharing up Jesus' clothing. After divvying up the clothes the underwear remains. John gives us a description of this item *"this garment was seamless, woven in one piece from top to bottom."* The soldiers do not want to tear up Jesus' underpants and agree among themselves to draw lots to see who would gain possession. Now, if we imagine Jesus as a humble man from the backwaters of the Galilee then his clothes couldn't be worth much, and after his previous beating the clothes would have been covered in blood and sweat – why then do the Roman troops want his underwear?

Like so many tales within the gospels, even the slightest details are inspired by the Jewish scriptures. Indeed, every detail of Jesus' last moments is given deeper

---

[98] John 19:23

meaning, even in the case of his underwear. John makes it clear that the soldiers want Jesus' clothes to fulfill prophecy from psalm twenty-two, *"They divided my garments among them and cast lots for my clothing."*[99]

The psalms are a collection of one hundred and fifty sacred poems that express various tenets of Judaism, which according to Jewish tradition were composed by King David himself. Psalm twenty-two elsewhere bears a striking resemblance to the death of Jesus, beginning with the line *"My god, my god why have you forsaken me?"* Are these similarities evidence that Jesus fulfilled the prophecies as many Christians assume, or are they evidence that the gospel writers pinched aspects of Jesus life from earlier texts?

We have already noted how reliant the gospel writers were on the Old Testament. They used the scriptures to find information about the life of Jesus because they believed his life was predicted in them. In this case, John has found inspiration from a psalm and applied it to the final moments of Jesus' life - he weaves the story of the soldiers wanting Jesus' clothing in order to 'fulfill' this psalm. We must, therefore, be wary of the historicity of this incident. After all, would Roman soldiers really want blood-soaked underwear, and for what purpose?

This story is so absurd it is best explained as an invention. If we accept the truth of the matter then we have to be even more careful about what the rest of the gospels are telling us of the death of Jesus. The events leading to his death are literally packed with theological interpretations, which make finding the historical truth behind why he died even more difficult. Nevertheless we do have evidence enough to make an historically plausibly argument regarding this matter.

---

[99] Psalm 22:18

Why Did Jesus Die?

The gospel narratives rely so much on ancient prophecies as a source of factual information about the life and death of Jesus, and are so clouded by theological bias that a clear picture of exactly why Jesus died is not immediately evident. His death is interpreted by the believers as being necessary for the redemption of humanity, and to this day we hear Christians claiming that Jesus died for our sins as part of a divine plan. According to Christians, Jesus was born merely to die.

The gospels ooze imagery supporting this notion, take for example when the Roman soldiers want to make sure Jesus had died, they elected to stab him with a spear rather than break his legs. The parallels with Jesus' crucifixion and the sacrificial lamb of the Passover festival become evident; the lamb was to be killed without breaking any of its bones as commanded by Mosaic Law. In this light, Jesus has paid the ultimate sacrifice for us. Jesus was the symbolic lamb.

Yet since so much Christian spin has accrued over the death of Jesus the historian must rightly question this explanation, neat as it is. In the Roman world, crucifixion was a horrid and humiliating punishment reserved for common criminals and rebels against Roman rule. Some scholars have pondered whether the scandal of a messiah executed like a common criminal led Jesus' followers to reinterpret the real reasons that Jesus was executed. They were so upset by his premature death that they began to see it as a necessary part of the plan. His death, instead of being an embarrassment, took on an altogether new meaning.

Meanwhile, a brief look through Jewish history of the period provides us with numerous examples of would-be messiahs who all met a swift end. Theudas had taken a crowd to the river Jordon promising to part it like Moses had done. Instead, he and his followers were mowed down by cavalry. Even John the Baptist, loved by the people, could not escape being beheaded by Herod friend of Rome. These examples serve to show how the authorities regarded charismatic men of the people. They were feared precisely because of their popularity. Did Jesus die for our sins as part of a divine plan, or did he die because he frightened the authorities? Which explanation is more historically plausible?

In the gospels, Jesus is followed by huge numbers of people. If he had managed to feed five thousand people then the authorities would have known about him. An entire Roman legion would comprise a very similar number of men and a mob of people following a single man during Passover, a time of potential riot, would have been enormous cause for concern. Additionally, if Jesus did himself have a political message, if his twelve disciples symbolized a redeemed Israel without Roman rule and if there were sword wielding Zealots and Sicarii among them, then plans might have been made to dispatch this man at once. Even if Jesus had no problems with the Romans, then certainly his criticism of the Sadducee temple priests and his overturning of the moneychanger's tables would have marked him out as a troublemaker. From the historical perspective, this explanation makes more sense as it fits so well into what we known happened to other charismatic religious leaders and it fits with what we know about the temperament of the Roman military in the region that it is the best explanation for why Jesus died. Jesus was executed, not for the redemption of humanity, but because he threatened the fragile peace.

Was Pontius Pilate Innocent or Guilty of Killing Jesus?

That Jesus was killed on a Roman cross is a fact of history, perhaps the only solid fact we have about his life. We know conclusively that crucifixion was practiced during Jesus' lifetime; we learn from Josephus that during times of insurrection it would be common to see thousands of rebellious Jews crucified by the sides of public highways. We also have archaeological evidence of a heal bone pierced by a nail dating from this period. We know that this Roman method of execution was reserved for criminals and rebels and that the Jews used stoning and beheadings to punish infringements of the law and Josephus contains several examples of the Jewish authorities practicing capital punishment. Jesus, therefore, was punished by the Romans and their leader in the region, Pontius Pilate. Yet this is not what we see in the gospels.

"I find no basis for a charge against him," John's Pilate says after interviewing the Galilean who had been handed over to his charge because, the gospels claim, the Jews have no right to execute him. Unwilling to execute this man, Pilate offers the crowd a choice. He says that there is a custom to release just one prisoner during the festival of Passover. *"Do you want me to release the king of the Jews?"* he asks of the crowd. Despite having miraculously fed thousands, and healed the sick, the Jewish crowds shout *"Crucify! Crucify!"* But Pilate answers, *"You take him and crucify him. As for me, I find no basis for a charge against him."* The Jews are insistent saying *"we have a law, and according to that law he must die, because he claimed to be the son of god.' When Pilate heard this, he was even more afraid, and he went back inside the palace."* The message of the gospels is clear - Pontius Pilate is innocent of killing Jesus.

Matthews's Pilate famously washes his hands of the incident to signify that he wants nothing more to do with the prosecution of an innocent man and it is the Jews who cry out *"his blood be upon us and our children."* For centuries after the Jews were blamed for their ancestors' crimes. In Europe during the Middle Ages, every time there was a plague or a missing child it was the "god-killing Jews" who were to blame. The fiercely Christian Europeans did, after all, have scripture on which they could base their baseless claims.

Can we exonerate the Jews for Jesus' death and make a case against Pilate? We know that Pilate was in Judea serving as the prefect during this time. This is attested by archaeological evidence in the form of a limestone block that was found during excavations of an ancient theatre in 1961. The Roman historian Tacitus also confirms that Pilate was serving at Judea in the capacity of the procurator. Despite the differences in the titles afforded to him it is evident that Pilate was the man in charge of Roman Judea from around 22-36 CE. Pilate was in the right place at the right time to have ordered the execution of Jesus, but is there any further incriminating evidence against him?

Josephus portrays Pilate as a man who is insensitive to the Jewish customs of the time. One incident records the Jews protesting over Pilate's use of Temple money. The Jews willingly donated monies for use in maintaining their beloved Temple. Indeed, it was a commandment of God that this tax should be paid. Pilate actually diverted this money away from the Temple and used it to fund the building of an aqueduct. Though the Temple would no doubt have benefitted from a decent water supply the use of this holy money sparked rage and crowds had assembled to protest. What did Pilate do to resolve this situation? Apologize and return the money? No, he disguised his troops and ordered them to blend in with the protesters in the crowd. When he gave a signal the soldiers revealed themselves and began to indiscriminately attack the protesters. Scores were killed.

Intriguingly, we also have other references to Pilate. Philo, writing to the Emperor Caligula, tells us that Pilate inflamed the Jewish population with his insensitivity to the Jewish laws of idolatry. Specifically, he hung up some votive shields in Herod's palace, which the Jews found abusive to their traditional customs because of the images on them. They were prepared to fight over the issue. Philo additionally describes Pilate as a man inclined to acts of abuse, while criticizing his *"successive executions of untried people, and his unending and incredibly vexatious cruelty."*[100]

Pilate, according to Luke, wasn't particularly fond of Galileans either, *"Now there were some present at that time who told Jesus about the Galileans whose blood Pilate had mixed with their sacrifices."*[101]

From the available evidence it is clear that Pilate was not a nice man. He held grudges, had a violent temper and was known for sending men to their deaths without trial. Would such a character have any difficulty in executing Jesus? The assembled evidence of the historical character of Pilate fits well with the fact that Jesus died on a Roman cross. Pontius Pilate, whatever the gospels tell us, is wholly responsible for killing Jesus and so the next step is to exonerate the Jews for this crime.

Why Were The Jews Blamed for Killing Jesus?

If Pilate is guilty then surely the Jews are blameless. To understand how the Jews came to bear all responsibility

---

[100] Philo, Embassy to Gaius
[101] Luke 13:1

for the death of Jesus one must first understand the environment in which the gospels were written. Mark, we should remember, is the earliest gospel, possibly written in Rome around the time of 65-70 CE. There are two important events occurring within the Empire that likely impacted on his gospel. The First Jewish War (66-70 CE) is raging between Jewish zealots and the Roman legions. Jewish patriots are unhappy with Roman rule in their lands, unhappy with taxation and unhappy with pagan religious practices in their monotheistic society. They will fight the Roman legions in a long, drawn out war that will ultimately culminate in the destruction of the Temple.

And in the great city of Rome on April 18th July 64 CE in the vicinity of the Circus Maximus a fire is breaking out. The Great Fire of Rome lasts for six days and seven nights and rages through the city. Temples, homes, shops and even the Emperor Nero's own palace is ravaged by the flames. In its wake, three districts of the city are utterly destroyed and seven suffer extensive damage while only four escaped unharmed. Some of the citizens are angry and blame Nero for the fire. It didn't help that he built a huge palace for himself amid the ruins. Nero instead blames the Christians. Tacitus tells us what Nero did to clear his name:

> "Consequently, to get rid of the report, Nero fastened the guilt and inflicted the most exquisite tortures on a class hated for their abominations, called Chrestians [ie Christians] by the populace. Christus [Christ], from whom the name had its origin, suffered the extreme penalty during the reign of Tiberius at the hands of one of our procurators, Pontius Pilatus, and a most mischievous superstition, thus checked for the moment, again broke out not only in Judaea, the first source of the evil, but even in Rome, where all things hideous and shameful from every part of the world find their

*center and become popular. Accordingly, an arrest was
first made of all who pleaded guilty; then, upon their
information, an immense multitude was convicted, not
so much of the crime of firing the city, as of hatred
against mankind. Mockery of every sort was added to
their deaths. Covered with the skins of beasts, they were
torn by dogs and perished, or were nailed to crosses, or
were doomed to the flames and burnt, to serve as a
nightly illumination, when daylight had expired."*[102]

Mark was undoubtedly influenced by these two events. If he did write his work in Rome then he would have been conscious that at any moment he could be sent into the arena for practicing Christianity. He was also quite aware that the Jews were causing trouble in the eastern fringes of the Empire. With these factors accounted for, his motivations for blaming the Jews for the death of Jesus become evident. Mark is trying to distance the Christians away from the Jews. In effect he is saying 'don't blame us Christians, it is the Jews who are always making trouble, look what they did to Jesus. Jesus was a good man, even Pontius Pilate could find nothing wrong with him.'

Mark tells us when Jesus breathes his last word a Roman centurion standing nearby exclaims, "*Surely this man was the Son of God!*"[103] It is significant that it was a Roman solider and not a Pharisee who proclaimed Jesus as the Son of God. Mark wants to show that the might of Rome should not have to worry about Jesus. His narrative makes it clear that the Jews are the real troublemakers, they killed Jesus and now they are starting a war. Yet the gospels cannot escape the one undeniable fact of Jesus' death, he died on a Roman cross and was not stoned to death by the Sanhedrin. The

[102] Tacitus, Annals XV.44
[103] Mark 15:39

gospels have to invent a sufficient explanation for how Jesus was ended up on the cross. The Jewish crowds are blamed for stirring trouble and to maintain order Pilate is forced to execute Jesus according to their demands. This of course is a historically unlikely explanation. Jesus had been popular among his fellow countrymen during his lifetime and Pilate was a brutal, insensitive leader who was more likely to send in his troops to violently disperse an agitated crowd.

Did Jesus Really Rise From The Dead?

Notions of a risen Christ, absurd as that may sound to modern ears, was a belief held by the very earliest Christians. These days, we are naturally skeptical of such miraculous occurrences, as we rightly should be, to avoid hoaxes like that of Daniel mentioned above. However, the first Christians quickly latched onto the powerful imagery of a man bought back to life, and indeed today this aspect of the Jesus story continues to be a very important, if not the essential, feature of Christianity. We should, therefore, seek to determine what actually happened in Jerusalem some two millennia ago.

In the case of Daniel, we saw how there was a strong belief in the possibility of miracles among certain sections of the Christian community in modern Nigeria. This underlying belief system makes is easier for some to accept that Daniel rose from the dead. We should therefore attempt to understand the attitudes that people in Jesus' time had towards the idea of the dead rising. To achieve this we should first examine something of the Jewish understanding of death from the centuries preceding Jesus' life.

In Old Testament times, there was no concept of heaven for the saints and hell for the sinners. Instead, a righteous and observant Jew could expect God to bless him with a long and healthy life in the earthly plain of existence. Conversely, the sinner would be punished by God for his misdeeds and could expect horrible diseases and various misfortunes in his lifetime. When death finally called to each man there was no afterlife to look forward to or fear. Instead every man, righteous and wicked, could expect to enter the murky realms of Sheol. This place, which is synonymous with its Greek counterpart Hades, offers nothing but a gloomy and godless existence with the soul existing in a state of endless slumber.

There were times, however, when it was possible to rouse one of these souls back to the realms of the living according to Old Testament traditions. Although necromancy was strictly forbidden in Jewish law, one story contained in the Book of Samuel illustrates that it was considered possible. King Saul is concerned that his enemies are near and seeks the service of a witch to assist raising a prophet so that he may know the future. The witch sees a spirit emerging from the ground, which Saul cannot at first discern. She tells him that she sees and old man in a robe, and then Saul recognizes Samuel. The risen prophet can speak and chastises Saul – it appears he didn't like being disturbed from his rest.[104] This example from the Jewish context, illustrates that sometimes at least the dead could rise again.

This understanding of the afterlife was evidently prevalent from a review of the Old Testament, but political events in the Second Century BCE would irrevocably change things. This was the era in which Antiochus and the Seleucids were forcibly imposing their rule in Israel (see the first chapter), a time when Judaism itself was under threat. Antiochus banned Jewish religious customs, a decision that would spark

---

[104] See 1 Samuel 28

the Maccabean revolt. Zealous Jews offered their lives in defense of their God but here came a dilemma. How could an observant Jew expect a happy and healthy life from God if he had offered it up at the altar of martyrdom? What was the point in dying for the faith if there were no rewards?

From this time forward there emerges a new concept in Judaism– the resurrection of the body, which finds an expression in Jewish literature of the time. The Book of Daniel, likely written shortly before or after the death of Antiochus, presents the concrete form of this new belief:

> *"Multitudes who sleep in the dust of the earth will awake: some to everlasting life, others to shame and everlasting contempt."* [105]

Two hundred years after Antiochus and the idea of resurrection for the just is still prevalent within Judaism but by no means universally held. Judaism in Jesus' period appears to have been split into two camps regarding belief in resurrection. The Sadducees, the conservative face of Judaism, Josephus tells us, were not believers in an afterlife and did not subscribe to the notion that the dead would rise again. Josephus also mentions that they expected no system of rewards or punishment after death. Their political and religious enemies, the Pharisees, however, did believe the dead would rise again. Interestingly, since the Pharisees would survive the trauma of the Roman wars they passed their belief in resurrection into modern Judaism. From an honest appraisal of Jesus' teaching and his focus on the Kingdom of God it is likely that he taught a set of beliefs similar to that of the Pharisees - Jesus believed that the dead would be bought back to life.

---

[105] Daniel 12:2

When Matthew describes the tombs of many holy men opening upon Jesus' death we can glimpse an ancient culture's certainty that the dead can rise. This incident is of course unlikely, it is mentioned only once in the gospels and there are no contemporary reports of dead saints roaming the streets of Jerusalem. Yet the example illustrates the culture into which ideas of a resurrected Jesus were based and is closely tied up with the Kingdom of God, a time when there would be a general resurrection.

The belief in resurrection and Jesus' own teaching provide fertile ground for resurrection stories to take hold shortly after Jesus' death. Some Jews were already open to the possibility of resurrection because there were incidents mentioned in the scriptures of prophets being able to raise the dead, both Elijah and Elisha for example were able to miraculously bring the dead back to life.

Outside of the Jewish context, there are also examples of belief in resurrection and the immortality of the soul. The ancient Greek literature is brimming with tales of heroes coming back to life and achieving immortality. Some were semi-historical persons who later became to be regarded as having divine power. The Greek historian Herodotus (circa 484 – 425 BCE), for example, mentions one Aristeas and his extraordinary life. According to this tale Aristeas, a poet, entered a shop and immediately dropped dead. The shopkeeper shuts shop and goes off to inform someone of the poet's demise. A traveler says that the shopkeeper must be mistaken because he had just now met Aristeas on the road and had even shared a conversation with him. When the family arrives to collect the body from the shop, they find the premises empty. Nothing happens for six years until Aristeas reappears again with a poem recording his exploits in a legendary land in the north.

He disappears again and appears several centuries later to instruct the citizens of a town to build a temple to Apollo.[106] Although there are similarities between Jesus and Aristeas it is not the content of the story that is important here. What is important to grasp is the willingness of the ancients to believe that a man could come back to life.

From a modern skeptical perspective, we know that it is impossible for a man to return after death but to an ancient pre-scientific society with minds full of mythological stories, the return of Aristeas makes sense – it fits in with their cultural expectations about what is possible. When the story of Jesus' resurrection first begins to make inroads in the Greco-Roman world, the pagans are receptive to the idea. This is the fertile ground in which stories of Jesus will take hold, grow and evolve.

In Luke's version of Jesus' resurrection appearance, two men are out walking on the road to Emmaus when they meet a stranger. They engage in conversation and invite the stranger to walk with them. They share the news of the executed Jesus, blaming the priests and rulers for his death. The mysterious man talks about why Jesus had to die according to the scriptures. They finally arrive at their destination and invite the stranger to stay with them. Suddenly, while breaking bread together, they realized the stranger was, in fact, Jesus! As suddenly and unexpectedly as he appeared, however, Jesus disappears, leaving the two men utterly bewildered.

The sentiment behind Jesus' mysterious appearances are best summed up by Matthew, *"when they saw him, they worshipped him; but some doubted."*[107] Matthew obviously records early strains of doubt among the Jews, even

---

[106] Herodotus, The History, Book 4
[107] Matthew 28:17

among some of Jesus' own followers. We can guess that many of the historical followers of Jesus did not believe the reports of his rising. The gospel writers incorporated tales of these doubters because they had to explain why many Jews of their period did not believe Jesus had risen. Furthermore, these doubters are used as examples for the faithful; they did not immediately believe what they saw but in the end, through faith, they saw the truth. This argument for having faith to believe Jesus still crops up today – but then again, faith can be used to justify belief in any number of gods.

By the time the gospels are written down ideas of a resurrected Christ were a firm conviction and a standard belief for many Christians. The resurrection came to be accepted as central to Jesus' teaching and a culmination of his time on earth. Of course Jesus did not physically rise from the dead according to our modern perspective, so how can these sightings be explained?

The murkiness of the sightings and additional stories like that of doubting Thomas, who did not believe Jesus had risen until he had actually inserted his fingers into Jesus' wounds, are interesting. The disciples did not immediately recognize their former master, which suggests that although Jesus was physically raised his appearance was altered somewhat. Then there are outright doubters. The message behind these incidents, the moral of the story if you like, is that faith is needed to recognize that Jesus has risen.

The followers of Jesus had given up their former lives to follow their master. These were a passionate group of zealous believers who fully expect the world to end at any moment. Suddenly and perhaps unexpectedly, their leader is arrested and executed but all of that passionate energy did not simply dissipate. It strove to find understanding in the shock and embarrassment of a dead leader. Mixed with their religious ideas of resurrection, some started actually experiencing Jesus again.

These were not objective sightings. All of the witnesses (as we shall learn) were already followers of Jesus who were suffering from the trauma of a beloved master killed before his time. Psychologically they are vulnerable and their visions reflect this uncertainty, but additionally they were already expecting the dead to rise based on Jesus' teaching to that effect. The believers, expectantly waiting for the kingdom to come were therefore already looking for signs that the Kingdom was coming. In their mourning, some witness shadowy and indistinguishable visions, and through faith, they understand this to be Jesus.

Conclusions

The exact reasons of Jesus' death cannot be known (unless some new evidence is found) but we can say with relative certainty that the gospel explanations for his crucifixion lack credibility. For various political reasons that were occurring during the time of the gospel writers, Jesus' death is blamed not on Pontius Pilate, but on the Jews themselves. Thus Jesus is executed because of the plots and plans of the Temple priests and the Pharisees.

The historical explanation of Jesus' death, as a potential troublemaker during a sensitive religious festival, fits better with our understanding of these times. Pilate was not a nice man and would have little problems with executing a rabble raising Galilean. This re-writing of history to serve the emerging Gentile church would have drastic consequences for generations of future Jews, who would, for centuries be blamed for killing God.

The shock of a leader executed in the manner of a mere criminal was scandalous enough for Jesus' disciples.

Although many of the disciples doubted the stories of his resurrection enough of them had faith in the strange, mysterious sightings to believe that this was Jesus returned from the dead. Perhaps this was the messiah after all, because hadn't Jesus talked of the Kingdom of God? Hadn't they been waiting for the stars to fall out of the sky at any moment? Weren't the dead supposed to rise when the Kingdom was coming? It must have made logical sense that these shadowy sightings were indeed the risen Jesus and evidence that his teaching was affirmed. Therefore, if Jesus' teaching was still relevant, hadn't they better continue preaching?

This apocalyptic cult of Jews represents the first roots of Christianity. Based on an understanding that Jesus was the messiah who had risen from the dead, they sought a continuation of their mission, which would take them into the lands of the pagans. It is in the Gentile world where the figure of Jesus develops into a fully fledged divinity, a process examined in the next chapter.

CHAPTER SEVEN

How Jesus Became God

The last person executed for their heretical beliefs was Cayetano Ripoll, who was hanged on the 31st July 1826. Ripoll had served in the Spanish army during the Napoleonic invasion but had been captured and interned in a French prisoner of war camp. During his time as a prisoner, he was exposed to new ideas, including some that were condemned by the Catholic Church. After his release, Ripoll returned to his hometown and continued his life as a schoolteacher.

It was his teaching that would lead him to trouble. Apparently, Ripoll had taught his students the principles of deism and had subverted these young minds away from the true Catholic faith. Deism itself was a product of the scientific revolution of the seventeenth and eighteenth centuries, and primarily taught that one could come to know God, not through faith alone, but through reason. Although there were many forms of deism, the main idea behind it was that God set up the laws of nature and then let the universe run on its own, God was a giant clockmaker who did not intervene with his perfect machine. Deism teaches that by studying the laws of nature (science) one can therefore know God.

We cannot be sure exactly what Ripoll taught, but it was evidently enough to land him in trouble with the Spanish Inquisition. Certainly by this stage of history the Inquisition had been in a steady decline but it still officially existed and was not finally abolished until 1834. When Christian kingdoms in the Middle Ages removed the Islamic Moors from the Iberian Peninsula, many Muslims and Jews had been forced to convert to Catholicism. The Inquisition began in 1478 as a means to ensure that these converts practiced orthodox Catholicism, but the Inquisition also moved into other areas. For example, it regulated which books were permissible and which were heretical but also defended the faith against witchcraft, blasphemy and sexual immorality. Of course, the Inquisition is best known for its horrific use of torture, and although the church never officially executed anyone, they had no qualms about handing the accused over to the secular authorities to finish the job. The favored method of execution was to burn the heretic alive.

At Valencia in 1826, Ripoll was hanged rather than burned, a reflection that society was moving on. To keep up with the gruesome tradition his body was flung into a barrel that was symbolically painted with flames. Europe by this stage was becoming increasingly secular thanks to advances in science, and Ripoll's execution was widely condemned.

From its earliest beginnings until today, Christianity has always sought to remain unified. The Inquisition sought to physically punish those who strayed from the orthodox teaching but throughout the church's history other means were employed to keep everyone singing from the same hymn sheet. The first missionary, Paul, warned his congregations against alternative teachings that were circulating at the very dawn of Christianity, and indeed as we shall see, there were in fact many diverse Christianities, each jostling for dominance over the others.

It is in this drive for unity that has shaped Christianity. Many of the very principles of Christianity were actually forged by arguments raging in the early church. The faith was won, not on the strength and authenticity of its teaching, but by a process of the survival of the fittest. This chapter will demonstrate that Christianity from its very beginnings was in a state of disunity and each sect sought to impose its version of faith as authentic, and in doing so, warped whatever message the historical Jesus actually had.

Years later, when the quest for the historical Jesus began, scholars were to attract controversy because by eliminating layers of theology laid down over centuries of Christian dominance, they were able to gaze at a Jewish rabbi of the first century as he actually was, rather than as he had been taught by doctrine. The historical Jesus was detached from Christian belief, he was alien to their assumptions, and it has since become clear that the idea of Jesus has actually evolved from his original context. Jesus had been born a man but came to be revered as the omnipresent God. This chapter will chart Christianity's early development and seek to comprehend how a humble Jew came to be preached as the creator of the universe.

What Did The First Disciples Believe?

We noted earlier how there were several charismatic leaders operating in the Jewish lands who were able to attract followers based on promise of performing miracles, and indeed Jesus can be seen in a similar vein, just like Theudas and the Egyptian, Jesus also attracted a band of followers. However, only Jesus' teaching survived. The fact is that there are no Theudasian Christians. Pontius Pilate and his Roman cavalry had put an end to these potential messianic movements before they ever began.

The Christian movement survived because of Jesus' original disciples continued preaching. The gospels tell us that they ran away at the moment of Jesus' arrest. Possibly, their fear of Pilate's retribution meant that they promptly fled the scene but in doing so they survived to tell the tale. Some may have returned to their former lives but others, scattered after their flight, began preaching a version of Jesus' teaching. From early on, there are numerous interpretations of Jesus and what his life and death represented.

The very first disciples of Jesus were Jewish in the sense that they observed the law, interpreted it and believed in a single God. Judaism was not a single entity in this era and the very first Christians were a small Jewish apocalyptic cult within a much broader context. Since Jesus is hailed as the messiah very early on, it is conceivable that these bands of men and women understood that Jesus was the man predicted by the scriptures and that his life pointed to the imminent arrival of the Kingdom of God.

Another important point to remember is, as Jews, these first disciples would not have regarded Jesus as God. All of that came later. Having said this, clearly they regarded Jesus as something beyond an ordinary rabbi of the period. Terms such as 'messiah' and the 'Son of God' while not indicative of divinity, certainly represented the first step towards Jesus' deification. By talking about Jesus in these terms the disciples clearly exalted Jesus above other teachers and prophets. In their understanding then, Jesus was already something more than an ordinary person. He was a man chosen by God to be a conduit for holy teaching, he was the latest of the prophets, and his life pointed to the expectation that God would intervene and establish his holy rule on this very earth.

Possibly, the term 'messiah' was applied to Jesus during his lifetime by his disciples, conceivably he may have even described himself in this way, but what does become apparent is that Jesus, upon his death, is given additional exaltation. The shock, humiliation and shame that the disciples experienced when their master was strung up like a common criminal was enough for some of them to want to explain it as indicative of some larger forces at work. Amid their passionate belief that the end was coming, that Jesus was the messiah, and amid the fear of persecution from Pilate, the disciples begin to experience Jesus again. Although the sightings are shady, they are enough to convince them that Jesus' teaching must continue. And for a group of desperate Jews they did a remarkable job because within four hundred years, Christianity would increase in popularity so that eventually even the Roman Emperors themselves would convert to Christianity.

How Did The Faith Spread?

The Jewish Christians, still practicing circumcision and interpreting the law, began to look to the lands of the Gentiles as the logical next step for their missionary activities based on an understanding of an ancient prophecy from the time of the Assyrians seven hundred years previously:

> *"And it shall be at the end of the days, that the mountain of the Lord's house shall be firmly established at the top of the mountains, and it shall be raised above the hills, and peoples shall stream upon it. And many nations shall go, and they shall say, 'Come, let us go up to the Lord's mount and to the house of the God of Jacob, and let Him teach us of His ways.'"*[108]

Closely associated in later times with the Kingdom of God was the idea that all nations would follow the God of Israel. The disciples who believe the messiah has come and the Kingdom was close may have been motivated to spread their message to all the nations

---

[108] Micah 4:1-2

based on this prophecy. In Matthew's gospel, Jesus commands the eleven remaining disciples to *"go and make disciples of all nations,"*[109] and this certainly supports this idea. Possibly, after Jesus died and the Kingdom did not come as expected the disciples opened their scriptures to seek answers and seeing the prophecy decided that Jesus' mission should be taken abroad.

We can be certain that there were early preachers in the name of Jesus who left the original confines of the Jewish lands and headed to the Roman Empire to spread their message. We know this because Paul was one of them, and from his letters there are references to other preachers out and about – who more often than not, present a message contrary to his own. Paul has to warn his congregations about these false teachers. From his letter to the Corinthians we hear of men coming from Apollos and separately Cephas (that is Peter.)[110] From this evidence it seems that a preacher had his own followings, and Paul thinks it is folly to boast about men in such a way. Evidently some of these teachers were still preaching about the necessity of circumcision for converts demonstrating that in its first stages Jewish Christianity was still prevalent. Paul warns against them, *"Watch out for those dogs, those men who do evil, those mutilators of the flesh."*[111]

Thus we can construct the dawn of Christianity as follows: Jesus' disciples and his early followers sought to convert the Gentiles, there were numerous missionaries but they were not part of a single movement and each had his own teaching. How would the Gentiles have received these new teachings from their Jewish contemporaries?

---

[109] Matthew 28:19
[110] See 1 Corinthians 3
[111] Philippians 3:2

The Romans had always been open to new religious movements. There is plenty of evidence that Roman citizens even attended Jewish recitals of the Torah in the numerous synagogues that were scattered through the Empire. The existence of this group is well attested through textual and archaeological evidence. This group, known as the 'godfearers', was free to learn about Yahweh and the Mosaic Law, although many would not have fully converted because of the requirements of circumcision. Circumcision would have been a painful and even dangerous procedure in a world without anesthetics or antibiotics, and generally the Romans were abhorred by the very idea. Circumcision, to their mind, was self-mutilation. Nevertheless, it is a testament to the open mindedness of the Empire that these uncircumcised godfearers were allowed to study religion from other cultures without threat of persecution or prejudice. It was entirely possibly for a godfearer to attend the Synagogue one day and sacrifice to a pagan deity the next; if they hadn't been circumcised then they were not bound by Mosaic Law and consequently were free to practice other forms of ritual observance.

The Romans were likely attracted to Judaism because it was of such an ancient age. The earliest scriptures dated back to the time of Homer and by learning about Judaism godfearers were partaking in something old, sacred and venerable. If the Romans were anything they were sticklers for tradition. When the first missionaries of Jesus were walking the roads of the Empire their message would have appealed to a broad range of people who would have been astounded by the tales of a man predicted centuries before coming back to life.

Traditionally, when the pagans wanted wealth, health or riches they turned to the gods, but when they harbored questions about the meaning of life and the substance of the soul they turned to thinkers such as Plato. Christianity, in its later stages especially, represented a unique package where a convert could find answers to questions and at the same time be hopeful for a better future. There was an added bonus in that they expected to gain life after death through accepting this new religion. Pagan religion was largely devoid of an afterlife, and the promise of resurrection would have been highly attractive.

Removing the constraints of Jewish law for potential converts as Paul proscribed opened the movement to everybody and anybody. New people bought in new ideas that would serve to transform the religion further away from its Jewish roots. In the creative mix of cultures and ideas a distinctly Jewish prophet with a distinctly Jewish teaching came to represent something more than a mere man. The Greco-Romans had a long tradition of deifying their great men and outside of his native context Jesus acquires himself a divine aspect, he evolves into a god, and then into God himself. By the time John writes his gospel, some sixty or seventy years after the crucifixion, Jesus is a fully-fledged deity. But John's example also demonstrates that Christianity had been influenced by Greek philosophy. The gospel of John equates the figure of Jesus with the everlasting logos, the governing principle of the cosmos, a term that had been in use since before Socrates. This was not something that was original to the historical Jesus. Jesus was a Jew and not a philosopher. Christianity found itself on fertile ground when it entered the Empire but its new surroundings further shaped it.

Arguably, it was men like Paul, who by spreading the gospel among the pagans had opened the floodgates. Since we have mentioned Paul numerous times throughout this book, we should now turn to his life as he is active in the period that we are examining.

Who Was Paul of Tarsus?

Paul (circa 5 BCE – 67 CE) is arguably the most important figure in the development of Christianity. Of the twenty-seven books of the New Testament, thirteen of them are attributed to him, although only seven are generally agreed by scholars to be genuine and the rest are undecided. If we say, however, that these texts were written by supporters or even students of Paul's religion we can say that almost half of the New Testament is Pauline in origin. These letters are revered as inspired scripture and form the very basis of the Christianity that we know today. Paul's influence is so strong that he is often described as the very founder of Christianity – he did more to shape its beliefs and practices than even Jesus himself!

Paul's letters are also vital for the historian because they allow such a fascinating and unique insight into the very first stages of Christian expansion. So who was Paul?

We can construct a picture of Paul not only through his own writings but additionally from the Book of Acts. Possibly written between 60 – 90 CE, Acts has been described as a biography, a history and even a novel. The author claims to have known Paul and even journeyed with him, but what is clear is Paul's central importance in this book. Various similarities in style and grammar make it likely that the author of Acts also wrote the gospel of Luke, and it is widely understood that both were written by a Greek-speaking Gentile, for a Gentile audience. Although there are numerous differences between what Paul writes about himself and his biography in Acts (in some places there are flat contradictions), we can nevertheless use these sources to paint a picture of Paul and the world in which he walked.

Paul, or Saul as he was originally called, was a contemporary of Jesus, born in Tarsus in what is now modern day Turkey. He tells us that he was Israelite of the tribe of Benjamin and a Pharisee also, and was educated under Rabbi Gamaliel - a Jewish teacher of the law well respected and honored by the people. Paul's education under Gamaliel places him in Jerusalem where he is in place to encourage the angry crowds to stone to death the first Christian martyr, Stephan, who had been condemned for speaking against Jewish law and the institution of the emple. By his own account, Paul was a very zealous Jew and he receives permission from the high priest to arrest the so called followers of the 'way' as early Christianity was known. As Acts tells it; *"Saul began to destroy the church. Going from house to house, he dragged off men and women and put them in prison."*[112] At this time, Paul seems more like a secret policeman in a fascist state than a saint of the Christian faith.

However, on his way to Damascus (circa 33-36 CE), Paul is struck by a startling light from the heavens above and a voice asks him *"Saul, Saul, why do you persecute me?"* He asks the identity of the disembodied voice, *"I am Jesus, whom you are persecuting,"* is the reply.[113] This is Paul's conversion to Christianity and from this moment onwards his zealous appetite for his Jewish traditions transforms and he becomes an equally passionate missionary in the name of Christ. The rest of his life is dedicated to preaching the gospel of Jesus, and his self-appointed mission will see Paul travelling extensively around the eastern half of the Roman

---

[112] Acts 8:3
[113] Acts 9:4-5

Empire, establishing congregations, quarrelling with other Jews, taking beatings and standing trial at the hands of regional governors. He travels throughout the eastern half of the Empire.

Around 49 CE, Paul is back in Jerusalem after his first missionary trip, where he meets with the Jewish apostles to discuss an important question, should the pagan converts need to be circumcised according to the law? Paul in his determination to allow all to accept the truth that Jesus has risen argues against it but evidently the Jewish apostles still favor it. James the brother of Jesus has the last say, *"It is my judgment, therefore, that we should not make it difficult for the Gentiles who are turning to God. Instead we should write to them, telling them to abstain from food polluted by idols, from sexual immorality, from the meat of strangled animals and from blood."*[114] Gentile converts therefore must still adhere to some important aspects of the Jewish law (for example kosher) but according to James' judgment they are free from the need to be circumcised.

During Paul's second missionary trip he finds himself in Corinth where he stays for over a year. It is at Corinth that Paul begins writing his famous letters. The first is addressed to his friends in Thessalonica where he established a congregation several months previously. This letter is the earliest of his writings to survive and certainly the earliest Christian document in the New Testament. In it he praises his friends in Thessalonica for turning away from idols and worshipping the living God. The tone of the work is friendly and encouraging but clearly he expects that Jesus will return again very soon.

---

[114] Acts 15:19-20

His very last trip across the seas is for a very different purpose. Acts tells us that when in Jerusalem in 57 CE to deliver some collected money for the Jerusalem church Paul is arrested for causing a disturbance. He is accused of bringing Gentiles into the Temple- an event that sparks a violent riot. The inner area of the Temple had traditionally been off limits to foreigners and the punishment for breaking this rule was death. The Roman troops arrest Paul for disturbing the peace, which ironically also serves to save his life from the angry mob.

The Romans are about to severely flog him for causing a disturbance when it is found out that Paul is a Roman citizen, which affords him certain legal rights. Now a prisoner of Rome, Paul is transferred to the provincial capital at Caesarea to stand before the governor of Judea. He spends two years in custody until a new governor reopens his case and accuses him of treason. Paul as a citizen of Rome appeals to the Emperor himself and is sent henceforth to the capital city. After this Paul is silent. Christian tradition has Paul being beheaded by Nero.

Paul was passionate and restless and his personality literally explodes through his writings. Fiercely defending his beliefs, the founder of Christianity hopes that the knife will slip for those who declare circumcision necessary, *"I wish they would go the whole way and emasculate themselves!"*[115] His fiery tempter emerges when he confronts Peter *"to his face,"* over his eating with the Gentiles. At the end of his letter to the Galatians, Paul grabs the pen from the hand of his scribe and in large bold handwriting warns his congregation to be wary of those in favor of circumcision.[116] Is this what he really told James and Peter? For in another letter he admits to being a panderer:

---

[115] Galatians 5:12
[116] See Galatians 6:11-18

"I make myself a slave to everyone, to win as many as possible. To the Jews I became like a Jew, to win the Jews. To those under the law I became like one under the law ... so as to win those under the law. To those not having the law I became like one not having the law...so as to win those not having the law."[117]

For Paul attracting converts is his mission and he doesn't mind bending a few principles here and there to win them over.

In his own mind, Paul is a unique man with a special mission that strikes as possessing a certain arrogance. At the same time he did make genuine friends and writes constantly to ensure they are well, and he is capable of great, thought provoking poetry. He speaks of love. He urges his congregations to unity. He is concerned with their salvation.

It is little wonder that his personality could both attract and repulse. His continual conflict with the Jewish Christians, including James, is defended by his belief that his version of the gospel is the correct one, he says *"I want you to know, brothers, that the gospel I preached is not something that man made up. I did not receive it from any man, nor was I taught it; rather, I received it by revelation from Jesus Christ."*[118] Jesus had taught James and the other apostles when he was still alive, so Paul's words here are a swipe at them. Paul believes that his version, because the risen Jesus taught it to him, is more authentic than that of the apostles.

Since by Paul's own account he has received his special teaching from something other than a human teacher, and since his influence on Christianity is immense, we

---

[117] 1 Corinthians 9:19-21
[118] Galatians 1:11-12

should, therefore, seek to understand just what was it he was teaching.

Did Paul Think Jesus Was God?

Christians have for centuries turned to Paul's letters to support their notions that Jesus was divine and even that Jesus was part of the trinity. However, if Paul really did conceive of himself as a Jew, which he does in certain passages, then he would not have worshiped Jesus as God. Indeed in none of his writings does Paul specifically state that Jesus is God.

Evidence for Paul's belief in the divine Christ is commonly cited in his letter to the Philippians. In his letter to this community of Macedonian Christians, Paul presents some sort of hymn. This hymn is unlikely to have been composed by Paul, because there are words in them that Paul does not use anywhere else in his letters and overall the grammar and style is alien to his own writings. Christians argue that as Paul did not compose the hymn then it is earlier than Paul. And since Paul was a very early Christian, here we are supposedly confronted with evidence that from very early on some Christians thought of Jesus as divine.

The hymn (if that is what it really is) does present a very divine sounding Jesus. Presented here is an extract of the hymn from the RSV translation of the bible rather than the NIV that has been used previously as it is a more accurate rendering of the Greek original:

> *"Let each of you look not to your own interests, but to the interests of others. Let the same mind be in you that was in Christ Jesus, who, though he was in the form of God, did not regard equality with God as something to be exploited."*[119]

---

[119] Philippians 2:3-8

This passage identifies Jesus as being in the 'form' of God and describes his equality with God. Naturally, it has been used as evidence to support Christian ideas that Jesus was essentially an aspect of God who appeared to humanity in human guise. Certainly, all historians will agree that Jesus came to be regarded as a divinity very early on, as this hymn shows, but does it reflect a belief of Paul's?

Throughout his letters, Paul often gives Jesus' name alongside God's, *"Grace to you and peace from God our Father and the Lord Jesus Christ."* This, however, does not mean that Paul thought of Jesus as God, merely that God and Jesus were important in his mission to be used in his greetings. In other places Paul is clear that Jesus was a man, *"by the grace of the one man, Jesus Christ"* who Paul also tells us was born of a woman, and was the seed of David.

In fact, the Philippians passage shows us what we already know, that there were numerous interpretations of Christianity in its early years, and some of these held Jesus in divine terms. Paul quotes the text, using the Greek word 'morphe' (form) to support a point he is making to the Macedonians; they should aspire to be humble just as Jesus was. The prime purpose of Paul quoting this hymn is not to support his notions of a divine Christ. Perhaps he used it to make a point to the Macedonians but it is unlikely that it supports his own beliefs. Paul also admitted to being somewhat of a panderer, so it would not be out of character for him to pander to the Gentile Macedonians (former pagans) by presenting this hymn with a divine Jesus.

Nowhere else does Paul describe Jesus in these terms. Christians should be cautious about proclaiming Paul's belief in the divinity of Jesus based on this one passage. And just because the hymn is early it does not necessarily follow that Jesus was God, as some

Christians have pointed out. It is interesting that this letter was presented to the Macedonians, who would have been familiar with Alexander the Great, the famous military leader also described in divine terms.

Possibly, the divinity of Jesus was proclaimed early on among the Gentiles, not only because there was a precedent for deifying great men in their culture, but also because the Jewish Christians were already describing Jesus in highly exalted terms such as 'messiah'. If God is omnipotent, if he knows ahead of time what he will do in the future and what its consequences will be, and if he had planned to send the messiah to the Jews then Jesus could be said to have existed eternally in the mind of God. From saying that the messiah had existed for all time in the mind of God, to saying he is actually an aspect of God himself, is only a small step away. Yet, if we were able to communicate with Paul and ask him whether he thought Jesus himself had a hand in the creation of the universe his Jewish upbringing would prevent him from providing an affirmative answer. Paul did not think that Jesus was God.

What Was Paul's Understanding of Jesus?

Skeptics have not been slow in pointing out that Paul, the founder of Christianity, never actually met in person the Jesus of history. Paul never knew or followed Jesus during his years on the earth, a claim that James and the Jerusalem church could justly boast. In quoting Paul as scripture Christians not only believe that Jesus rose from the dead, but also specifically they believe that Jesus appeared to Paul.

For a man who claimed a direct teaching from the resurrected Jesus and a man who had never personally known Jesus it is not surprising that Paul very rarely references any of Jesus' actual words. Whereas the gospels are packed with parables and sermons, Paul never mentions them. Indeed, despite his status as the earliest Christian writer Paul's letters give us no additional details about the life of Jesus.

Nevertheless, he is proud to boast in his special status and evidently regards himself as an apostle with a mission given to him by the risen Jesus to preach to the Gentiles. What he preaches is perhaps best summarized in his own words:

> "For what I received I passed on to you as of first importance: that Christ died for our sins according to the Scriptures, that he was buried, that he was raised on the third day according to the Scriptures, and that he appeared to Peter, and then to the Twelve. After that, he appeared to more than five hundred of the brothers at the same time, most of who are still living, though some have fallen asleep. Then he appeared to James, then to all the apostles, and last of all he appeared to me also, as to one abnormally born."[120]

Paul places himself on the list of those to whom Jesus appeared. The others on this list presumably all knew Jesus personally. This speaks volumes for how Paul perceives himself and his own mission; in placing himself on this list he is assuring us that he is equal with the other apostles. This list also demonstrates that Jesus appeared to only Jews and only to his own followers. Jesus did not for example appear to the ruling Emperor, to Josephus or any objective witnesses, which would have made his resurrection truly miraculous. Therefore, Paul's example shows us that at the preliminary stages Christianity was essentially a continuation of a Jewish sect.

Thus, although Paul the Jew hold Jesus to be a very exalted person, and more than a mere man, his vision of

---

[120] 1 Corinthians 15:3-8

Jesus still lacks its essential divinity that will be assigned to him by later Christians. For example, Paul says *"By his power God raised the Lord from the dead, and he will raise us also"*[121] Notice that he says that God raised Jesus (the Lord) from the dead, not Jesus raised himself from the dead.

Paul does declare Jesus to be the 'Son of God', which of course means one thing to a Jew and another to a Gentile. By the time Paul refers to this title it is already closely associated with the messiah and perhaps synonymous with it. Jesus died on the cross and after his resurrection the title was firmly fastened onto him. Thus the 'Son of God' meant the 'messiah', the one whom God had chosen, but at this stage of history there was still no understanding that the bearer of the title was omnipresent.

For Paul, however, it is the resurrected Jesus that is the most important aspect and his vision of Jesus on the road to Damascus does influence his teaching. Overall, there is an almost obsessive fixation with the meaning of the cross and Jesus' re-birth. This is evident even in his understanding of baptism. Paul, in his own words, explains the meaning of baptism, submerged and then raised from the water, just as Jesus died and rose again, the convert has died and risen anew. The baptismal pool is the tomb, the water is the spirit. The body of the newly baptized is like Christ himself and one should therefore abstain from sexual immorality and sin for fear of corrupting it. Paul's obsession with the death of Jesus is apparent in this analogy.

Additionally, in Paul's letters we begin to see the doctrine of atonement being transformed. The Jews had always understood that sins could be forgiven through

---

[121] 1 Corinthians 6:14

a combination of repentance and temple sacrifice. For Paul, Jesus died for our sins and through faith in Jesus and maintenance of a sinless life the converts can expect to live into the new era. *"That if you confess with your mouth, 'Jesus is Lord,' and believe in your heart that God raised him from the dead, you will be saved."*[122]

Paul's letters also preserve the imminent expectation that a sudden and drastic event will shatter the known world, the same event that Jesus referred to as the Kingdom of God. Again this represents a continuation of a Jewish sect's understanding that the world is about to change, but for Paul is has added meaning. Paul writes to the Thessalonians to reassure the brethren there:

> *"Brothers, we do not want you to be ignorant about those who fall asleep, or to grieve like the rest of men, who have no hope. We believe that Jesus died and rose again and so we believe that God will bring with Jesus those who have fallen asleep in him. According to the Lord's own word, we tell you that we who are still alive, who are left till the coming of the Lord, will certainly not precede those who have fallen asleep. For the Lord himself will come down from heaven, with a loud command, with the voice of the archangel and with the trumpet call of God, and the dead in Christ will rise first. After that, we who are still alive and are left will be caught up together with them in the clouds to meet the Lord in the air."*[123]

According to Paul's view expressed above, he fully expects to be alive when Jesus makes his second trip to earth. What is interesting is that this concept of resurrection is still in its infancy at the time of his writing. Only those who have accepted Jesus can expect to experience resurrection. It is only later that the doctrine

---

[122] Romans 10:9
[123] 1 Thessalonians 4:13-17

of a general resurrection and the judgment of all mankind is written into Christian theology. Those who had not heard the message of Jesus would remain dead in Paul's view, and this understanding of Jesus' second coming may help to explain the urgency of his travels.

"For I tell you that Christ has become a servant of the Jews on behalf of God's truth, to confirm the promises made to the patriarchs so that the Gentiles may glorify God for his mercy, as it is written..."[124]

After this statement, Paul lists several relevant passages of prophecy relating to the Gentiles accepting the God of Israel. Paul as a Jew wants to be an instrument of God's will by preaching the good news of the messiah to these nations. Thus Paul's mission is framed to the Gentiles. Once the gospel is preached among them (which he clearly states is his purpose) then the Kingdom will arrive and the pious among them, those who had accepted Jesus, would rise to live again.

When we see Paul's dramatic life, his adventures abroad, his fighting with the Jews, we can imagine a man who wants to complete his goals before time runs out. He wants to save as many people as possible because he knows that time is short and those who did not accept Jesus will be missing out on the new life.

Perhaps Paul realized that if his Gentile congregation believed Jesus was a God then they would follow him all the more stringently. As a Jew he would have been prevented from believing this himself, but if it allowed him to save more souls then all the better. This is mere speculation of course but we turn now to this issue and seek to determine when Jesus was first understood to be divine.

---

[124] Romans 15:7

When Did Jesus First Become Divine?

So, Jesus was a Jew who taught his fellow Jews about the Kingdom of God – itself an inherently Jewish idea. Yet Christians regard him as something different entirely. Jesus is a part of the Holy Trinity comprised of the Father, the Son and the Holy Ghost; three distinct aspects of a single God. Jesus, as one of these aspects therefore would have had a hand in the very creation of the universe itself. Clearly, the image of Jesus has undergone quite a transformation from his original Jewish self all the way to his status as the Christian God. The historical Jesus wasn't regarded as a God in his own lifetime, even Paul never calls Jesus God, and yet he is worshipped as one today. How then did he come to hold this status?

It is likely that Jesus becomes to be regarded as divine when the earliest Jewish followers of Christianity began to spread their message into the predominantly pagan lands. Unlike the Jews of the period, the Greeks and Romans had numerous deities, and indeed some of them, for example Asclepius, had started out life as an historical person but through time had acquired a divine understanding. Could the same process be at work with the case of Jesus?

Christians have claimed that this is not the case. Their argument goes that the period from Jesus' death until the time that the gospels are written is only a short amount of time, and certainly not enough time for Jesus to accumulate legendary aspects. Therefore, because Jesus is hailed as divine very quickly then we are supposed to believe he really is a God and that people in his own lifetime recognized him in this way. This argument is nonsense.

In the Book of Acts, a remarkable incident is recorded which is directly relevant here. The apostle Paul and his colleague Barnabas are in Lystra, a town that would now be located in Turkey. Paul is preaching with passion and fervor so that one man who had never walked in his life suddenly jumps to his feet.

"When the crowd saw what Paul had done, they shouted in the Lycaonian language, 'The gods have come down to us in human form!' Barnabas they called Zeus, and Paul they called Hermes because he was the chief speaker. The priest of Zeus, whose temple was just outside the city, brought bulls and wreaths to the city gates because he and the crowd wanted to offer sacrifices to them."[125]

From this incident it is interesting to see how rapidly the ancients could attribute divine powers to men of the earth, even men they had just met. As soon as the lame man jumped to his feet the priest had already bought animals to sacrifice to Paul and Barnabas. All of this presumably took place in a matter of hours. Would a people so inclined to see the divine have any trouble accepting that Jesus was from the heavens?

In this story Paul protests about this treatment, he is after all just a man. Well, first century Jewish Christians also considered Jesus a mere man, a special man indeed, the messiah perhaps but still just a man. To the pagan Gentiles, however, there was nothing in their cultural background that prevented a belief that a man could attain divine status. Good Roman citizens, for example, offered sacrifices to the Emperors for the good health of the Empire and no one stopped to questions this practice. The Senate officially voted to deify the great Julius Caesar and encouraged its citizens to remember him through sacrifices, yet he was a mere man. It would, therefore, seem that much of the divinity of Jesus can be attributed to the influence of the pagan

---

[125] Acts 14:11-13

Romans who increasingly heard the story of an extraordinary Jewish man with miraculous powers.

Meanwhile, there are all kinds of similarities between pagan rites and early Christian rituals, which some scholars say, illustrate the influence of paganism on Christian religion. Jesus offering bread and wine as a symbol of himself in the last supper for example strikes us as being remarkably similar to the ritual practices of cult of Mithras in which bread and wine were also ritually consumed. If we are correct in understanding the pagan influence of Christianity, then why didn't Jesus' original Jewish followers stand up to complain?

We do know that Jewish followers of Jesus remained in Jerusalem after their master had died, among them was James. The church of Jerusalem is shown to have been important in the age of Paul. James is later killed in 62 CE and shortly after, the Roman legions sack Jerusalem in 70 CE and the Jewish church was effectively wiped from the map. It seems the turbulence of these times ripped out the main center of early Christianity and as a consequence there was simply no centralized Jewish-Christian stronghold to counter pagan claims of Jesus' divinity. Jewish Christians would survive for centuries but the main focus of their version of Christianity no longer boasted the power it once had. There was nothing to stop the idea of Jesus evolving in the Gentile world. There was no one strong enough, like James, to point out that revering Jesus as a God was essentially an abhorrent act of idolatry and an affront to Jewish monotheism.

Given the strict Jewish sensibilities when it came to monotheism, we can say that the historical Jesus likely kept within these confines. He was a Jew preaching to fellow Jews with a Jewish message. The vast Jewish crowds depicted in the gospels would never follow a man who claimed to be God. They would not have left behind families and friends because their teacher was contravening the very basic and most revered principles of Judaism. Jesus was not a God in his own time but practically as soon as his name is uttered among the lands of the Gentiles, just a couple of decades after his death, Jesus becomes divine.

What Was Paul's Influence on Alternative Christianities?

In these early days of Christianity there were many diverse understandings of the faith. Mostly we know they existed because some of the church fathers wrote about them precisely to denounce them. We hear of the Nazareans, the Montanists, the Gnostics, the Ebionites, the Arians, to name but a few. Each of these sects believed that their version of Jesus was correct, because no religion exists based on the premise that they are offering false teaching.

Meanwhile, Paul's importance as the founder of Christianity cannot be underestimated. He did more to spread the movement than anyone else, but without a solid theology behind him, his words were open for interpretation. There was only one Paul, and because he thought that time was running short he never bequeathed to the world an exact theology or doctrine, and so there were many diverse faiths who claimed him as their own. Below we shall examine several early versions of Christianity that are now extinct and their attitude towards Paul, which will adequately illustrate that from its very beginnings Christianity was fractured into competing faiths.

MARCION

Marcion (circa 85 – 160 CE) was born the son of a bishop in Sinop, now in northern Turkey which in those days was under the control of Rome. Marcion is described as having made a large fortune in his town, possibly he was a ship owner or a ship builder, but not much is known about his early years because later writers would regard the movement that he inspired as heresy. Epiphanius, an Orthodox Church father who wrote a compendium of heresies from his own time, informs us that although in his youth Marcion led a life of chastity and asceticism his sinful seduction of a virgin led to him being expelled from the church. This incident likely represents a later slander against Marcion, with the girl in question representing the purity of the church that Marcion had corrupted. Either way, Marcion leaves his hometown and travels to Rome and quickly gets involved with the church there. He immediately makes a splash with the Roman congregation by donating a huge amount of money to the church. His gift would have certainly made his name known among the congregation, but Marcion was not content with merely distributing monies. He had bigger ideas.

Marcion seems to have established his own interpretation of Christianity around the year 144 CE. He was quite familiar with the texts of the Old Testament but recognized that the God portrayed therein was not the same God that Jesus and Paul had preached. The God of the Old Testament was prone to extreme punishments for those who could not keep the laws that he had established. In Marcion's view, the apostle Paul taught that a person is distinguished by his acceptance of the gospel of Christ and not by following the law. Jesus, in Marcion's opinion, came into this world and paid the penalty of mankind's sins and thereby saved us from the wrath of the Old Testament God. Marcion says that there are actually two gods, the vengeful god of Israel and a more peaceable and compassionate heavenly father that Jesus taught.

Consequently, he rejects all of the Jewish texts as a product of an evil deity.

Marcion believed that above all, Paul was the most important apostle of Jesus. When Jesus appeared to Paul on the road to Damascus he did impart some special teachings, which allowed Paul to know the truth. Truth that only he was privy to and a truth that the Jewish Christians could not know. When Paul confronts the Jewish apostles, James and Peter, he is clearly in the right because of his unique relationship with the risen Christ.

Based on an understanding of Paul's letters, Marcion interprets Jesus in a docestist manner - put in another way, Jesus was not mere flesh but appeared in a form that only mimicked the human body. Paul's statement that Jesus came *"in the likeness of sinful flesh,"*[126] would have certainly inspired Marcion's views on the matter. These ideas would spark massive outrage by those who preached that Jesus had a body of flesh and that he really did suffer on the cross.

Marcion suggested his own canon of the bible, in which Paul's letters took center stage. He also used a version of Luke, but purged it of all references to the Old Testament and the Jewish religion. This proved immensely popular and for many years Marcion and his movement were serious rivals to the emerging Catholic Church, which had to move to sharply address this problem.

Although condemned as a heretic, Marcion, in fact, had a massive impact on the development of the Catholic Church. It was his idea to form a canon of accepted texts in the first place and his radical ideas of the nature of Jesus quickly spurred the Catholics into solidifying their own accepted dogmatic rules of belief, which led to the

---

[126] Romans 8:3

development of the Trinity and an acceptance that Jesus was flesh and bone, but divine also

VALENTINIUS

Another strain of Christianity that challenged the status quo was inspired by Valentinius (circa 100-160 CE), who, like Marcion, had expounded an alternative understanding of Jesus from the great city of Rome. Born in the Nile delta at a place called Phrebonis, Valentinius gained a Christian education from a certain Thuedas, who claimed to have himself received secret teachings from no one less special than Paul himself. These teachings were passed on through master and student, and naturally Valentinius was the inheritor of this tradition.

Tertullian in his work 'against heresy' mentions that Valentinius wanted to become bishop of the Roman church and that he possessed eloquence of speech and a sharp mind. As such, he was described as a good teacher and may have even enjoyed a prominent role in what would become the Catholic Church - except that he subverted its teachings. Tertullian says that Valentinius began to preach an alternative and dangerous teaching after he was refused the position of bishop.

The movement that he inspired can actually be considered alongside several other similar movements that collectively are known as the Gnostics. The term Gnostic derives from the Greek word for 'knowledge' and in this sense refers to the secret knowledge passed on through the chain of apostles. In this case Jesus gave secret knowledge to Paul, who taught Thuedas, who taught Valentinius.

Although there are numerous similarities between the Gnostic groups they are actually all independent from each other. They are also difficult to understand because of their complex theologies and hidden, secretive ideas. In general the Gnostics borrowed largely from Greek philosophical reasoning and were particularly inspired by Plato. Gnostics, like Valentinius looked out at the world and saw that it was not perfect, there was disease and injustice for example, and they reasoned that the creator of the material world was himself not perfect. Thus, borrowing terms from Plato the God of the Old Testament became associated with the Demiurge – a deity that was responsible for creating the material world. This was not the only supernatural intelligence at work in the universe because above the Demiurge, at the center of everything stood the primal father, known as the Bythos. The Bythos was considered the highest god, a perfect spiritual being from which the various layers of reality emanate.

The Gnostics understood Jesus within the context of neo-platonic thought. Jesus himself originated from one of these Bythoric emanations and descended to the material world in the guise of the savior of humanity. Through understanding Jesus, we can, therefore, comprehend a higher truth. This Gnostic reasoning represents an amalgamation of two cultural ideas and serves to illustrate the fertile ground in which new ideas could take hold in the Roman Empire of this period.

Valentinianism was perhaps the most eminent of the Gnostic groups, having a widespread following that ranged across the Empire, with a substantial congregation residing in Rome itself. Practitioners of this secret knowledge differed somewhat from the other early Christians because they could attend services and ceremonies in other churches and even in the emerging Catholic Church. A practitioner of Valentinianism, or any form of Gnostic teaching, would have been indistinguishable from any other person singing in the church, although they would be privy to special knowledge that the others did not know.

This was unacceptable however. The surviving literature from the first three centuries of Christianity is full of contempt and slander against these Gnostics and their false teaching. This did not stop the Gnostic groups from spreading and exerting an influence throughout the period of the early church. Valentinianism would survive well into the fourth century and with it a high opinion of Paul.

What Did The Jewish Christians Think About Paul?

As we noted earlier the Jewish Christians were an important movement at the very center of early Christianity. Being Jews, the Jerusalem church initially deemed it important that even Gentiles be circumcised. What is clear from Paul's writings, however, is that the Jewish Christians centered in Jerusalem do wield a certain level of power and influence, and even Paul went to Jerusalem to present his version of the gospel before the pillars of the church. Only Paul's version of events survives in his writing and in Acts, which makes it clear that James and Peter blessed Paul's work, but in reality we do not know James' true reaction. Paul's often arrogant high regard for his own gospel makes is likely that this is not the whole story. We must look beyond the New Testament to understand what Jewish Christians might have thought about Paul.

There is a series of writings called the Pseudo-Clementines that survive in two distinct forms; the Homilies and the Recognitions. These two traditions likely rely on an older text and like the gospels they have undergone a period of modification and editing and are written for theological and not historical motives. Epiphanius bishop of Salamis (circa 320 – 403 CE) mentions that the Clementine literature was in use in his lifetime by the Jewish Christian sect called the Ebionites.

The works represent an understanding of Christianity from a Jewish-Christian perspective. For example, they call Jesus the *'true prophet'* which matches with what we might expect a Jewish Christian to say about Jesus. More to the point, Peter in the Homilies says; *"Our Lord neither asserted that there were gods except the Creator of all, nor did He proclaim Himself to be God."*[127] Clearly the Ebionites who revered the text were still monotheists by nature.

Paul's name doesn't actually appear in the Clementines. Instead, the name Simon the Magus is used synonymously with Paul's. Anyone familiar with biblical history will recognize Simon as the same man who appears in the Book of Acts; he is a nefarious magician who thinks he can pay to learn the secrets of the miracles performed by the apostles. He is, therefore, the first heretic. Despite the name change, the similarities with Paul's life are often strikingly obvious in the texts. It seems the author of clement was actually slandering Paul by comparing him with the heretic Simon.

In one scene, Paul, in the guise of Simon, is debating with Peter who argues that the Jewish law is still valid. Remembering that Paul attained his special teaching through a revelation, Peter in the Homilies attacks him:

> *"But can any one be rendered fit for instruction through apparitions? And if you will say, 'It is possible,' then I ask, 'Why did our teacher abide and discourse a whole year to those who were awake?' And how are we to believe your word, when you tell us that He appeared to you? And how did He appear to you, when you entertain opinions contrary to His teaching?"*[128]

---

[127] Homilies 16.15
[128] Homilies 17.19

According to the Homilies, Peter is the correct interpreter of Jesus and Simon (Paul) has corrupted the message. His point is that the original apostles knew Jesus when he was alive and that they had at least a year together before he was executed. Of course the Clementine literature is late, heavily edited and interpolated, yet they serve to illustrate that not everyone was fond of Paul and that some sought a continuation of Jewish Christianity even as late as 360 CE.

Unfortunately, for reasons that will be explained shortly, the Jewish Christians were by this stage overshadowed by a far greater force. As for the original Jerusalem Church of which all the evidence points to James being the leader, it did survive but only for a short time. Being located in Jerusalem would have disastrous consequences for James' church. After the failed Bar Kokhba Revolt (132-136 CE) the Romans destroyed the city and banned any Jews from setting foot inside again. This edict applied equally to the Jerusalem church because its members were still Jewish. The church historian Eusebius records that after the revolt there were only Gentile bishops presiding over the church.[129] We can assume that with its central power removed, and an increasingly diverse understanding of Christianity spreading through the Empire, the revolt had been the last blow against Jewish Christianity. Of course, as the Pseudo-Clementines illustrate, some Jewish sects would continue to teach, but now they had no political standing and had to compete with a movement that was growing in power – the emerging Catholic Church.

---

[129] Eusebius, Historia Ecclesiae, 4:6

How Was The Battle of Faith Won?

The groups surveyed above serve to remind us that Christianity was in no way a single entity in its earliest stages. Paul had come across competing preachers in his own time and even though there was only one Paul, there were numerous groups who held numerous opinions about him. Evidently, the original message of Jesus was being lost amid all these competing voices.

Yet from among these groups, one began to stand out and overshadow the others. This movement will grow into what will be ultimately known as the Catholic Church. Renowned scholar Bart Ehrman has termed the emerging catholic faith of the second and third centuries as the proto-orthodox church. More than any other sect of this period, it is the conflicts emerging between the proto-orthodox and the alternative sects that created the character of the fully developed Catholic Church. Additionally, internal conflicts within the movement bequeathed to us Catholicism in its recognizable form. It is the successors of the proto-orthodox who finally decided on which books were canonical (scripture) and which were heretical (for example Paul was authentic while the Pseudo-Clementines were heretical), thus we arrive at the modern bible, as we know it. Through much wrangling and argument, it was the proto-orthodox that gave future generations the 'correct' interpretation of Jesus and his relationship to the father and the Holy Ghost (theology). It was the proto-orthodox who provided us with the Eucharist – the eating of bread and wine as a symbol for the body of Christ and the practice of Baptism (ritual). And they determined the exact hierarchy of the church, with a pope at the top, bishops below and deacons at the bottom.

That we can proclaim the proto-orthodox as victorious can be argued because it is the version of the faith that is favored and ultimately selected to be the official faith of the Roman Empire in 380 CE. Previously, there had been much heated debate about Jesus' divinity and his relationship with the father. These issues were finally settled at the Council of Nicaea in 325 CE. Today, the vast majority of Christian denominations declare themselves to be Trinitarian and this is a direct result of the council and its official proclamations.

The road to Nicaea had been a difficult one. In the second and third centuries, the proto-orthodox movement was in no shape or form a single entity, and none of its theology and ritual was standardized, and there was no guarantee that the proto-orthodox would be victorious against the numerous alternative Christianities. And some early proto-orthodox writers were later rejected as heretical by the successors of their tradition. Origen, (185–254 CE) who wrote one of the first philosophical analyses of Christianity was popular in his day but deemed heretical in the sixth century by his successors.

At some point, Christians revered a divine Jesus alongside the divine God. Additionally, there was another aspect of God known as the Holy Ghost, or Holy Spirit, which was described in the Old Testament (in Hebrew the Ruach HaKodesh) as emanating from God and influencing the world in numerous ways. For example, in Genesis, God's spirit provides life. In the second century, some sects of Christianity came to revere each of these three concepts as being divine and for the first time the term 'trinity' is coined.

The development of the trinity possibly owes a large part to pagan religion where it was often the case that three gods were worshipped as one. Plutarch (circa 46 –

120 CE) a Greek philosopher of the middle-platonic school in his work 'Moralia' describes a trinity of deities from Egypt (Osiris, Isis and Horus). *"Osiris may be regarded as the origin, Isis as the recipient, and Horus as perfected result. Three is the first perfect odd number."*[130] Plutarch mentions the inherent power of triangles and the perfection of the number three and this is the arguably the roots of the Christian trinity.

Debate, however, quickly emerged over the exact nature of this trinity. Was one element superior to the other or were they all equal? Perhaps the most heated argument was whether Jesus was 'homósousía' or 'hómoiosousía' – or in English, whether Jesus was the same substance as God as understood by the proto-orthodox, or whether he was of a similar substance to God, as understood by the Arius.

Arius (circa 250–336 CE) was an Egyptian born Christian who came to teach that the father had created the son. This teaching was popular and widespread yet the competing proto-orthodox were thoroughly disgusted by it. They held that Jesus had not been created but had always existed alongside the father. The Arian controversy caused a split among the church. A council was convened at Alexandra in 321 CE and Arius was declared heretical and was expelled from the church. Yet Arianism did not disappear after that.

The issue could only be resolved by the personal intervention of the Emperor Constantine I. Having come to power in a divided Empire ruled by two emperors, Constantine recognized the need for unity. He had to fight off his challengers and had successfully reunited the Roman Empire under his own single rule. Although he was himself a pagan many of his subjects were

---

[130] Moralia, 5:26

Christian and he saw the political need for religious unity. Christianity could be the 'glue' that united his Empire. By having an active hand in this religion Constantine was perhaps envisaging a future where he could further control his subjects. This was the first time the state would intervene with religious matters.

It was Constantine who convened the meeting at Nicaea precisely to figure out whether there was an 'io' or not in Jesus' relationship with his father. The meeting favored the dominant proto-orthodox view and the Nicaean creed (although later revised) is still recited in churches today. The Nicaean meeting paved the way for the church to be officially sanctioned as the state religion. All other understandings were henceforth heretical and indeed Arius and several other bishops were banished.

What Factors Contributed To The Victory?

From its Jewish origins to its neo-platonic reinterpretation, the understanding of Jesus was extremely varied. We are therefore justified in questioning how one group gained superiority over the others.

Ironically, perhaps, the winner was able to succeed and transmit its version through a process of the survival of the fittest. It was not the strength of ideas that counted; it was the strength of the people who harbored them that did. After all, the Jewish Christians likely possessed a more authentic teaching than did the proto-orthodox but they were in no position to assert their authority after the fall of Jerusalem.

The key to the proto-orthodox victory lies more in its political organization. Originally, when Paul wrote his letters he addressed them to the entire congregation, because in the early years, Paul's communities lacked leadership. Possibly, Paul thought that time was running out and therefore organizing an effective hierarchy was pointless. However, a few years later Jesus still hadn't returned and now there was much internal squabbling and disagreement among the communities. In the absence of clearly defined leaders, the congregations were running amok; we hear of lawsuits, drunkenness and adultery in Paul's churches.

By the time The First Epistle to Timothy is written, however, things are changing. This epistle, dated between 130-150 CE is written in Paul's name (actually it is a forgery by a person who revered Paul). In it we discover that some among the congregation at Ephesus stood up to take charge, and the epistle, therefore, sought to codify church organization and assign defined roles to the bishops and deacons.

Strong leadership allowed the 'correct' transmission of teaching to new generations and it allowed the church to defend itself against alternative ideas. This was something that the Gnostics, being by nature a secretive sect, did not have. The Gnostics believed that everyone had an equal opportunity to study the secret teachings and it was up to the individual and not the institution to find the answers.

The presence of a strong hierarchy later assisted the church to settle on an authentic version of Christianity – at least 'authentic' as the proto-orthodox perceived it. In fact, there was a strong trend towards finding a universally acceptable faith. The word 'catholic' actually does mean 'universal.' Although early on there was no universal faith the various epistles and homilies dating to the second and third centuries show that there was a concerted effort to produce one. The surviving texts show the bishops of far-flung churches in constant communication with each other. Among these works we hear of appeals to flock to unity and flee from division.

The proto-orthodox clearly saw the need for unity and strived to achieve it.

The proto-orthodox used their system of hierarchy to bolster their claims of true and authentic teaching. They argued that at the beginning of the chain was Jesus who passed his knowledge to the disciples and apostles who in turn passed it onto to the first bishops. The idea was that a bishop passed on his teaching to his successor who passed it on to the next. Today, the Catholic Church still argues their authenticity by claiming Peter, an original disciple of Jesus, as the first bishop of Rome.

Naturally, other sects claimed they had received authentic teaching but the proto-orthodox took it a step further. Theirs was the true version and the others had simply misunderstood Jesus' teaching or worse were deliberately out to subvert his true message. Indeed, the writings of the proto-orthodox go to great extents to blacken the name of the heretics, accusing them of everything from holding orgies to being perverted from the truth by the devil.

Ignatius' words against the Jewish Christians demonstrate the polemical high horse adopted by the proto-orthodox: *"Never allow yourselves to be led astray by false teachings and antiquated and useless fables."*[131] The proto-orthodox knew they were correct because at the end of the day they were willing to die as martyrs during the persecutions. The nefarious Gnostics avoided it at all costs because only believers in the truth were willing to die for their beliefs. In the orthodox understanding martyrdom was affirmative proof that they were right. As such martyrdom was encouraged. Ignatius on his way to Rome for public execution writes ahead to the Christians there pleading with them not to interfere, he

---

[131] Ignatius, letter to the Magnesians

writes *"Fire and cross and packs of wild beasts, cuttings and being torn apart, the scattering of bones, the mangling of limbs, the grinding of the whole body, the evil torments of the devil – let them come to me, only that I may attain to Jesus Christ."*[132] The Gnostics however had their own opinion about the matter. A work discovered at Nag Hammadi dates from the era of the persecutions and records a Gnostic attitude towards martyrdom. According to their view, these willing martyrs were fools who because of ignorance seek death: *"If the Father were to desire a human sacrifice, he would become vainglorious."*[133]

So, the proto-orthodox had a set of internal governance that fostered unity and the transmission of teaching from generation to generation, but perhaps there is another reason that assisted their victory on the road to Nicaea. Rome.

In antiquity, Rome was the greatest city that had ever stood. All roads lead to Rome and certainly those same roads meant that there was a Christian community there before 64 CE. There is a text that was once regarded as scripture but was later rejected, known as 1 Clement. Despite not making it into the Canon, this letter is, in fact, an early Christian document dating from around 96 CE. The Christians at Corinth, whose fathers would have known Paul, had ejected their leaders and installed others in their place. Clement, the then Bishop of Rome, writes to the Corinthians to sort this problem out; he urges them to leave their disunity behind and reappoint their former leaders. From this letter, we can see two geographically distant churches in communication with each other. What is fascinating, however, is that it is the Church of Rome who are concerned with their brethren in Greece. Rome as the

---

[132] Ignatius, letter to the Romans
[133] Testimony of truth

center of political and military power in its age is precisely the kind of place where one church can grow to dominate all others and impose its own teachings.

Conclusions

Jesus' urgent calls for the Jews to reform before the Kingdom of God arrived sparked a movement that would quickly spill beyond the borders of Galilee and Judea. The first missionary trips into the Empire were by Jews who likely understood the conversion of the Gentiles as a pre-requisite for the Kingdom to come. At this stage Christianity was still very Jewish in its nature.

Paul had witnessed the resurrection of Jesus and also went to the lands of the Gentiles in order to preach. He fought for his beliefs with passion while denouncing his competitors in the process. In Paul's understanding, all men, both Jew and Gentile, through a faith in Jesus could attain an afterlife in the imminent resurrection. He sought to remove the constraints of circumcision from potential converts and was prepared to argue his case with the pillars of the Jerusalem church. Since he believed that he would live to see the resurrection he did not bother with writing an exact theology – he was instead determined to bring as many converts as possible into the faith before the catastrophe arrived. The influx of new converts meant an influx of new ideas and new interpretations. Few of the former pagans would have had any difficulty in understanding Jesus as divine and very soon indeed Jesus was described in divine terms and still the end never came.

The proto-orthodox, who were mostly Gentiles themselves, took the message of Jesus and made it their own. As the church gained strength, other faiths were swallowed up or deemed heretical by the proto-orthodox bishops. The original Jewish Christians were lost in the sands of time, condemned by the victors as heretics and evildoers. Today, the two billion Christians owe their understanding of God to a long process of historical evolution solidified at the council of Nicaea with the support of the Roman Emperor. Ultimately, it was political power that shaped Christianity today.

The Evolution of Faith

Jesus began life some two thousand years ago in the Galilee. We know nothing historically certain about his birth and early life other than speculating what it must have been like for a young man living like his contemporaries in a Jewish world coming under increasing Roman influence. At some stage, Jesus begins to teach. What he taught has to be carefully reconstructed because centuries of mythalization has created something that he could not possibly have been, but modern scholars unanimously recognize Jesus as a Jew of the first century. His movement likely represented a single Jewish sect among a diverse mother religion and he differed to some of his contemporaries in his expectation of an imminent and drastic end of the world order as they had known it.

This was based on an understanding that God, speaking through his prophets, would set aside a single man to be the anointed one. Some Jews expected the messiah to be a great military leader of a type similar to Bar Kokhba who would reunite Israel through holy war. Some of these ancient prophecies also talked about a time when the Gentiles, who in the past had treated the Jews with contempt and conquest, would come to celebrate the God of Israel. The age of Jesus was colored by messianic and apocalyptic expectation.

Jesus begins his career in this climate. He wanders the lands preaching to other Jews but also healing them and exorcising their demons. Of course, this was hardly extraordinary because there were other men who were understood to have performed miraculous deeds, but

Jesus was somehow different; Although the majority of Jews may have paid little attention to this upstart from the backwaters of the Galilee, Jesus did form a core of ardent and zealous followers around him who were willing to leave behind their families and livelihoods in order to follow him in preaching the way. Most likely it is their expectation that the Kingdom would descend within their lifetimes that provided their mission with such apparent urgency.

Eventually, Jesus leaves behind his native Galilee and heads towards Judea. He enters Roman occupied territory and heads towards the very epicenter of the Jewish religion, the Temple at Jerusalem which at that time was brimming with pilgrims who had come to celebrate the festival of the Passover. The Jewish festivals in the Roman period were often large powder kegs into which politics and religion combined to make a most explosive mixture. The Roman overseers and their Jewish collaborators were extremely wary during these times when many hundreds of thousands of Jews descended upon a small area. Jesus, with all his talk of new kingdoms, at a time when politics and religion were indistinguishable, certainly worried the authorities. Pontius Pilate, who had a dreadful reputation for antagonizing the Jews, for executing them without trial and for sending his cavalry to cut down popular leaders, had absolutely no qualms about crucifying Jesus. Jesus is arrested by the Temple authorities and handed over to Pilate. Underneath Jesus' dying corpse the sarcastic epitaph *'king of the Jews'* made Pilate's opinion of Jewish liberty crystal clear.

The disciples had run away when Jesus was apprehended and history shows that none of them were crucified along with their master. Perhaps they were ashamed by their actions, perhaps they were stunned that their beloved leader had been so easily done away with but in a period of reflection some among them would witness a murky figure standing nearby. Hadn't Jesus also believed that the dead would rise when the kingdom came? Wasn't this a sign that they should continue Jesus' work? Wasn't there a prophecy that all nations would one day follow God?

Jesus' execution does not stop the movement that he inspired. His followers decide instead that his tragic death was actually part of a larger plan of God's and the Kingdom really was coming. They understood Jesus to be God's anointed favorite who had pointed to the time when heavenly justice would rule over the earth. To some, the land of the Gentiles was the logical next step for proclaiming Jesus and the Kingdom.

Although the Romans had sometimes shown themselves to be intolerant of Jewish sensibilities in their rule of Judea, generally speaking they were open minded to new gods and certainly throughout the Empire the Jewish religion was tolerated and even protected by the state. The Romans, for example, had made special efforts to protect the temple tax donated by Diaspora Jews from pilfering hands, and Jews were exempt from pagan religious obligations to the state gods that other citizens were required to perform. Probably, at this earliest stage, few Romans would have been able to distinguish a Christian from a Jew. But it was among the pagans that Christianity found a willing audience.

Meanwhile, Jesus' very own flesh and blood brother took over the movement as the head of the Jerusalem church and Jewish Christianity remained stationed outside of the Temple for a brief time. Indeed, some thirty years after Jesus' death this movement is still centered in Jerusalem, which demonstrates that it was still essentially a Jewish sect. James was certainly familiar with the Jewish missionaries who were active in spreading the message and he certainly knew of Paul.

Paul had witnessed the risen Christ himself and taken it upon himself to preach the gospels among the Gentiles. Years later, he finally arrives at Jerusalem to seek the blessings of James and the other pillars of the Jerusalem church. There is a conflict here because Paul believes that his Gentile converts should be free from the obligations of Mosaic Law, especially regarding circumcision. That Paul has to argue his case so passionately demonstrates that at this time the Jerusalem church were still expecting certain aspects of the law to apply to all. Paul believes that the time is extremely short and that he can save many more people if they do not have to undergo circumcision. Although we cannot know for sure what transpired at this meeting, Paul and his supporter Luke makes it clear that James gave his blessings; Gentile converts need not be circumcised but they should still observe elements of the kosher law and abstain from the abhorrent worship of idols which contravened the very basic tenants of Judaism.

Missionaries like Paul were responsible for bringing the name of Jesus to the Empire. In many of the great cities there were already communities of Jews, and even some Gentiles attended the services at the synagogues to learn about the Jewish God. The idea that Jesus was the messiah attracted some of the Jews and godfearers but Paul's abrasive personality and his certainty that the Kingdom was coming appalled many – Paul is often chased out of towns or suffers a terrific beating. Certainly the message that he preached, that the world was about to end a controversial one and offended many. Nevertheless, Paul does establish several communities of believers in cities such as Galatia and

Corinth, and he writes letters to his friends there to keep them following his version of the gospel. There are other missionaries who will visit them and these newcomers often tried to 'subvert' Paul's work by claiming that converts must be circumcised in accordance with the law.

When Paul is active, Christianity is still an offshoot of a minority Jewish sect, but freed from the obligations of circumcision the movement attracts new blood from among the pagans. They are attracted to the idea that Jesus was in fact the fulfillment of ancient Jewish prophecies and that by following Jesus they can hope for an afterlife in the Kingdom of God. Certainly this was a more attractive option than a desolate afterlife in the shadowy realms of Hades. The Gentile Christians rejected their old gods made of wood and stone in favor of the one true God of Israel and his messiah.

For centuries, the plethora of pagan gods had maintained the peace and security of the Empire. The Empire had bought order to chaos, and had civilized the barbarian nations. By rejecting the divine patrons of Rome the Gentile Christians were accused of being un-Roman. By shunning the traditional gods they were inviting divine wrath. When a massive fire erupts in Rome it might have seemed that the gods were furious that the Christians were turning against them. Nero found an easy scapegoat for the fire and began to persecute this vile new movement by setting them alight to watch them burn in the night. This was but the beginning of the persecutions. Future generations of Christians would be sent to the beasts of the arena as punishment for rejecting their gods – they were executed as atheists!

A few years after the first persecutions and the original disciples are beginning to die out and their oral teaching was under threat of extinction. There was a need to record Jesus' original teachings. Somewhere within the Empire, the first Christian scholars began to record what they had heard spoken about Jesus several decades previously. At first they write down lists of all his sayings but later still these sayings are incorporated into the broader context of a story that detailed the life of Jesus. The first among the canonical gospels was Mark. He writes during the first traumatic persecutions at Rome and amid a scene of building war as the Jews are beginning to foment revolt against Roman rule in their homelands.

Other gospels writers will come, each own with its own spin on the Jesus story. Some gospels are more Jewish than others. Some are more Hellenistic in nature. Each reveres Jesus as the messiah. But the earliest gospel in the bible has a recognizably human figure of Jesus. However as the faith gradually permeated through the former pagan lands it is colored by that culture so by the time John is writing Jesus is already proclaimed as a god and his gospel reflects this. Among the Gentiles there had always been a tradition of ascribing divine powers to extraordinary men, and to their minds Jesus, with his great moral teaching and miraculous healing ability must have shared some aspect of the divine. And since the father knew in advance everything that would occur through history then he must have conceived of the messiah's earthly mission from the very beginning of time. The idea of the messiah had pre-existed in the mind of God. With thinking like this it would only need an additional step for Jesus to merge with the father and to become an actual aspect of the creator being, existing from time immemorial and active in the governance of the earthly realm. Christianity by this stage had finally and irrevocably splintered from its mother religion.

By the time of John's gospel, there already are many competing and alternative gospels and many interpretations of Jesus and his relationship to the father. Some of these Christianities had sought to remain Jewish, others had in fact rejected everything Jewish about their religion, some blended seamlessly with neo-platonic thought to create the numerous Gnostic movements. Christianity was contradictorily varied and lacked any regulating body. New movements sprung up everywhere. In the coming centuries these numerous sects, which all claimed Jesus as their figurehead, will battle it out for dominance. In their desperate bid for superiority, these Christians are probably not aware that they are pulling Christianity further away from the historical message of Jesus. They are shaping Christianity according to their own concerns and the product will ultimately be something new and unrecognizable.

In proclaiming Jesus to be God, these Christians encounter several problems, because for one thing Jesus as a Jew was a monotheist. Jesus had prayed to the father, to the one God of Israel, but in doing so was he merely talking to himself? The Gentile mind had long been influenced by Greek philosophy and it was only natural that reasonable thinking of the philosophers should be applied to questions of Jesus' exact nature. Indeed, Philosophy and Jewish religion found a unique synthesis in Christianity. But the interpretations were vast, and with nothing less than eternal salvation or damnation, the arguments were heated. The correct interpretation of faith was necessary for salvation and yet there were already so many different versions. Each claimed to be definitive. Each claimed special teaching from the apostles.

Two hundred years after the crucifixion the idea that Jesus was actually a third aspect of God emerge and early conceptualizations of the trinity are found in Christian writing. Of course, this idea was not universally accepted but took hold among a group of Christians labeled as the proto-orthodox. Eventually this movement, with its drive to find unity, and its desire to establish a strong hierarchy emerge as the politically most powerful Christian movement.

Constantine I, Emperor of Rome, saw the need for unity among the Christians and the need for an official and accepted doctrine, so he convened a conference of bishops and strived to hammer out a deal between the squabbling Christians. Eventually, through the political motivation of fostering unity, the trinity is accepted as the only true understanding of Jesus. From now on, any faith professing a different belief system will be branded as heretical. The Council of Nicea made it abundantly clear that Jesus was God and any other teaching was prohibited.

Jesus was born a man but he had evolved into a God. When historians, two thousand years after his death, got down to the business of searching for the historical Jesus their results would prove controversial. By cutting though centuries of Christian theology and searching for the very beginnings of Jesus, they saw a man as he was, and not as he had been preached from pulpits all over the world. Seen without his cloak of two thousand years of Christian doctrine, the historical Jesus seemed strange, alien almost. Indeed some historians have even rejected the notion that Jesus ever existed at all, and although their reasoning is wrong, it is easy to see how they came to their conclusions.

Now that we have seen how historically a Jewish rabbi came to be God let us now, as an adventure in speculative question making, attempt to resurrect the historical Jesus from the grave. With the conclusions that we have postured regarding Jesus' Jewishness and his re-constructed mission, let us ask our resurrected Jesus what he thinks about everything that has been done in his name.

As a Jew, the historical Jesus would have been strictly monotheistic and strictly against idolatry so what would he think of all the carved statues of himself and his mother Mary? What would he think of the generations of men and woman kneeling before these statues and offering prayers? What would he think about all the paintings, Christmas cards and movies? Christianity, as practiced today, is a direct contravention of the very fundamentals of the Mosaic Law and Jesus the Jew would likely be horrified.

Would our resurrected Jesus have been disappointed by the fact that the Kingdom of God, as he would have taught, still has yet to descend on the earth? His prime motivation in the synoptics seems to be to warn his fellow Jews that shortly God would destroy the present world order and establish his own heavenly kingdom on this very earth. He, therefore, called his people to repent, to turn towards God, and change their lives for the better in preparation. Yet two thousand years later Christians are still waiting for the dead to rise from their graves. Does this make the historical Jesus a false messiah as he himself would have defined the term?

What would he think about the Catholic Church's historic rise to power and its accumulation of massive amounts of wealth? What would he make of the monolithic churches and golden alters dedicated to him? He himself was a humble man born in a region of farmers and fishermen and all the evidence points that he had rejected material wealth. And yet today there are numerous preachers who by selling their books and DVDs hope to not merely support themselves and their family but become rich in the process.

Today, the shape of Christianity owes little to the actual teaching of the historical Jesus, but more to Christian theologians who continued to interpret (Jesus might say distort) his message. Christianity did not splinter away from Judaism, it evolved away, and Christianity will continue to evolve, that much is certain. Today, there is a bewildering array of Christian denominations, each one representing a response to prevailing social conditions of the age. Did Jesus teach that female clergy were permissible? No, because this is a question arising from our own age and not his. Yet as western morals progressed and realized that men and women really are equal, society has reflected back on the church and sought to impose modern standards on it, so that today it is perfectly acceptable to listen to a female member of the clergy in the Anglican Church.

Did Jesus teach about the evolution of life forms? Of course not, as a Jew he would have accepted that God personally created all beings, and at first the Catholic Church continued with this frame of mind. At the first Vatican council in 1870 this conclusion was reached:

> *"Hence all faithful Christians are forbidden to defend as the legitimate conclusions of science those opinions which are known to be contrary to the doctrine of faith."*

But as science continued to prove infallible, and one hundred and fifty years of supporting evidence made it clear that Darwin's theory was actually fact, the church was forced to change its attitude. During the International Theological Commission in 2004, Cardinal Ratzinger, now better known as Pope Benedict XVI endorsed the following statement:

"Since it has been demonstrated that all living organisms on earth are genetically related, it is virtually certain that all living organisms have descended from this first organism. Converging evidence from many studies in the physical and biological sciences furnishes mounting support for some theory of evolution to account for the development and diversification of life on earth."

The attitude towards science in the church has changed according to the prevailing conditions in society. As religion is a human invention it is therefore not surprising that it is influenced and shaped by human society. Religion must change to survive. It must adapt to the environment that it lives in. Religion really does evolve. And there is no doubt that as long as people continue to worship Jesus he also will continue to transform.

Recommended Reading

For those who are interested in studying more about the historical Jesus I can particularly recommend reading: *"Jesus: Apocalyptic Prophet of the New Millennium"* by Bart Ehrman, *"Jesus of Nazareth: King of the Jews"* by Paula Fredriksen, *"Jesus the Jew,"* by Geza Vermes or *"The Historical Figure of Jesus"* by EP Sanders. Or if you are interested in some other aspects covered in this book the following list might prove useful.

Allison, Dale C.,
- *"Jesus of Nazareth: millennium Prophet"*
- *"Resurrecting Jesus: The Earliest Christian Tradition and its Interpreters"*

Blackman E.C. *"Marcion and His Influence*

Boyd, Gregory A. *"Cynic Sage or Son of God: Recovering the Real Jesus in an Age of Revisionist Replies."*

Boyer, Paul, *"When time shall be no more"*

Brandon, S. G. F. *"Jesus and the Zealots"*

Brown, R.E., *"The Death of the Messiah"*

-*"The Virginal Conception and the Bodily Resurrection of Christ"*

Chilton, Bruce, *"The Temple of Jesus: His Sacrificial Program within a Cultural History of Sacrifice"*

Cohen, Shaye J.D. *"Respect for Judaism by Gentiles According to Josephus"*

Collins, John J. *"The Sceptre and the Star: The Messiahs of the Dead Sea Scrolls and Other Ancient Literature."*

Crossan, J.D., *"The Historical Jesus: The Life of a Mediterranean Jewish Peasant"*

-*"The Birth of Christianity: Discovering What Happened in the Years Immediately after the Execution of Jesus"*

Dart, John and Ray Riegert, *"Unearthing the Lost Words of Jesus: The Discovery and Text of the Gospel of Thomas"*

Dickson, John, *"Jesus: A Short Life."*

Dunn, James, *"The Parting of Ways Between Christianity and Judaism and Their Significance for the Character of Christianity"*

Ehrman, Bart D.

- *"After the New Testament: A Reader in Early Christianity"*
- *"Jesus: Apocalyptic Prophet of the New Millennium"*
- *"Jesus, Interrupted: Revealing the Hidden Contradictions in the Bible"*
- *"Lost Christianities: The Battles for Scripture and the Faiths We Never Knew"*
- *"The New Testament: A Historical Introduction to the Early Christian Writings."*

Elledge, K.C.D., *"Life after death in early Judaism: the evidence of Josephus"*

Evans, C.F., *"Resurrection and the New Testament"*

Finegan, Jack, *"The Archaeology of the New Testament"*

Fredriksen, Paula, *"Jesus of Nazareth: King of the Jews"*

-*"From Jesus to Christ. The Contribution of the Apostle Paul."*

Funk, Robert W. *"Honest to Jesus: Jesus for a New Millennium"*

Funk, Robert W., Roy W. Hoover, and the Jesus Seminar. *"The five gospels."*

Gager, John G., *"The Origins of Anti-Semitism: Attitudes towards Judaism in Pagan and Christian Antiquity."*

Grant M., *"Jesus: An Historian's Review of the Gospels"*

Gray, Rebecca, *"Prophetic Figures in Late Second Temple Jewish Palestine"*

Habermas ,Gary R., *"The historical Jesus: ancient evidence for the life of Christ"*

Hengel, Martin, *"Was Jesus a Revolutionist?"*

Hick, John, *"The Myth of God Incarnate"*

Hurst, L.D., *"The Epistle to the Hebrews"*

Jackson, Ralph, *"Doctors and Disease in the Roman Empire"*

Johnson, Kevin Orlin, *"Why Do Catholics Do That?"*

Johnson, Paul, *"A History of the Jews"*

Koester, Helmut, *"Ancient Christian Gospels: Their History and Development"*

Kummel, W.G., *"Introduction to the New Testament"*

Lane Fox, Robin, *"Pagans and Christians"*

Lüdemann, Gerd, *"Paul: The Founder of Christianity"*

Mackey, J.P., *"Jesus, the Man and the Myth"*

MacMullen, Ramsay, *"Christianizing the Roman Empire AD 100-400"*

McKnight, Scot, *"A Light among the Gentiles: Jewish Missionary Activity in the Second Temple Period"*

Metzger, Bruce M., *"The Text of the New Testament: Its Transmission, Corruption, and Restoration"*

Nickelsburg, George W.E., *"Jewish Literature Between the Bible and the Mishnah"*

Ogg, G., *"The Chronology of the Life of Paul"*

O'Leary, Stephen, *"Arguing the Apocalypse: Toward a Theory of Millennial Rhetoric"*

Pagels, Elaine, *"The Gnostic Gospels"*

Perrin, Norman, *"Jesus and the Language of the Kingdom"*

Rajak, Tessa, *"Josephus: The Historian and His Society"*

Riches, John, *"Jesus and the Transformation of Judaism"*

Roukema, Riemer, *"Gnosis and Faith in Early Christianity: An Introduction to Gnosticism"*

Rowland, Christopher, *"Christian Origins"*

Rusch, William, *"The Trinitarian Controversy"*

Sanders, E.P.,

- *"Jesus and Judaism"*
- *"Paul"*
- *"Paul and Palestinian Judaism"*
- *"The Historical Figure of Jesus"*

Segal, Alan F.,

- *"Rebecca's Children: Judaism and Christianity in the Roman World"*

- *"Life after death: A History of the Afterlife in Western Religion"*

Smallwood, E. Mary, *"The Jews under Roman Rule"*

Smith, Morton, *"Jesus the Magician"*

Stark, Rodney, *"The Rise of Christianity: A Sociologist Reconsiders History"*

Taylor, Joan E., *"The Immerser: John the Baptist within Second Temple Judaism"*

Tiede, David L., *"The Charismatic Figure as Miracle Worker"*

Vermes, Geza,

- *"Jesus the Jew"*
- *"The Authentic Gospel of Jesus"*
- *"The Dead Sea Scrolls: Qumran in Perspective"*
- *"The Religion of Jesus the Jew"*
- *"The Resurrection"*

Wilken, Robert L., *"The Christians as the Romans Saw Them"*

Wilson A.N., *"Jesus a Life"*

Yoder, J.H., *"The Politics of Jesus"*

STAY INFORMED

Please visit the author's blog for more intriguing
articles on the subjects of faith and reason...

www.god-proof.com/blog

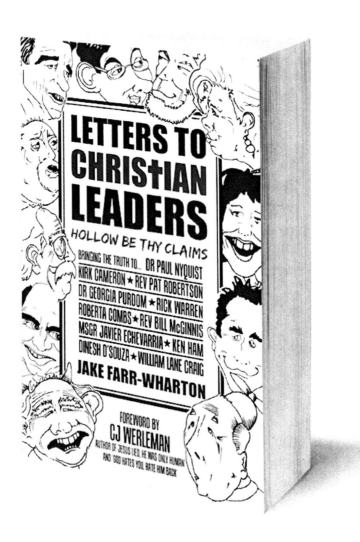

EXPLICIT CONTENT
WARNING
HARMFUL TO FAITH

HE WAS ONLY HUMAN
CJ WERLEMAN

Lightning Source UK Ltd.
Milton Keynes UK
15 March 2011

169308UK00001B/2/P